£1.18

Withdrawn

Photomicrographs of the non-flowering plant

Photomicrographs of the non-flowering plant

A. C. Shaw
Head of the Biology Department, The Skinners' School, Tunbridge Wells

S. K. Lazell, A.R.P.S.
Medical Photographer, Tunbridge Wells Hospital Group

G. N. Foster
Junior Research Associate, School of Agriculture,
University of Newcastle-upon-Tyne

LONGMAN

Longman Group Limited
London

*Associated companies, branches and representatives
throughout the world*

First published 1968
Second impression 1971
ISBN 0 582 32550 1

Printed in Great Britain by
William Clowes and Sons Limited, London
Beccles and Colchester

Contents

Preface and acknowledgements   vii

Algae   8–21

Fungi   22–31

Lichenes   32–33

Mycorrhiza   34–37

Bryophyta-Hepaticae   38–45

Bryophyta-Musci   46–49

Pteridophyta-Lycopodiales   50–65

Pteridophyta-Filicales   58–65

Gymnospermae   66–79

Index   80

Preface

The aim of this book is basically the same as that of the companion volume, 'Photomicrographs of the Flowering Plant'; to present to students of Botany and Biology at Advanced Level a set of photomicrographs of the structure and reproduction of as wide a range of flowerless plants as they will meet in their initial studies, side by side with labelled diagrams from which they can interpret what they can see under the microscope.

We have, wherever possible, deliberately used slides of the same standard as those normally available to schools and we realise that no single photograph of a portion of material on these slides will show as much as the student can see for himself under the microscope. We have had to decide what to show in the photograph focusing at a certain depth. We hope that the drawing which accompanies each photograph presents most of the detailed structure which the student will see for himself on the slide.

The photographs were obtained with a Beck London 47 microscope and eyepiece camera using Ilford Micro-Neg. Pan. and HP3 film. The drawings were obtained by drawing over a faint print with Indian ink and bleaching out the photograph. For certain of the living preparations we have used the technique of phase-contrast microscopy. We did this to demonstrate structural detail which does not photograph satisfactorily under the light microscope.

We would not ourselves expect our students to make drawings of organisms such as *Chlamydomonas* and *Euglena* but we would expect them to make careful observations of the living organism slowed down with, for example, brilliant cresyl blue. From these observations they can obtain the information in the drawings. Future studies lead on to the examination of electron-micrographs and we have exemplified this approach with an electronmicrograph of *Chlamydomonas*.

A. C. Shaw

Tunbridge Wells, 1967   S. K. Lazell

G. N. Foster

Acknowledgements

We are grateful to the following companies for the provision of slides: T. Gerrard and Co. Ltd., Flatters and Garnett Ltd., Harris Biological Supplies Ltd. and Northern Biological Supplies. Living material was supplied from the Culture Collection of Algae and Protozoa, Cambridge. Our special thanks are due to Mr. T. A. Gerrard who at one time in the preparation of the book allowed us to borrow any slides from his complete collection, Mr. R. R. Fowell for advice on yeast morphology, Dr. W. Richards for the loan of slides, Dr. F. A. L. Clowes for his slides of beech mycorrhiza, Mr. Martin Lazell for assistance in the collection of living material, and Mr. R. A. Boulding for contributing hand-cut sections to our collection of preparations.

Fig. 35 (bottom right) is reproduced from a photograph by the late Dr. D. W. Ivimey-Cook in McLean and Cook *Textbook of Theoretical Botany*, Vol. I, Longmans. Dr. George E. Palade, of the Rockefeller Institute, New York, kindly provided us with fig. 2, the electronmicrograph of *Chlamydomonas*.

Mrs. Lazell deserves our best thanks for both her encouragement and her forbearance.

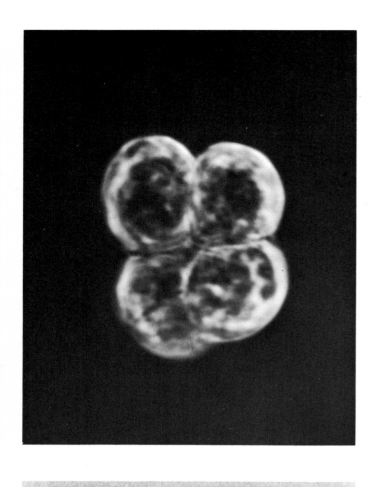

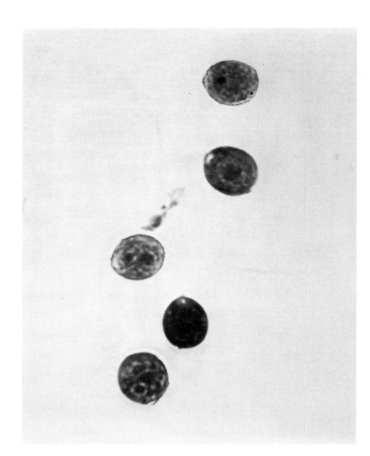

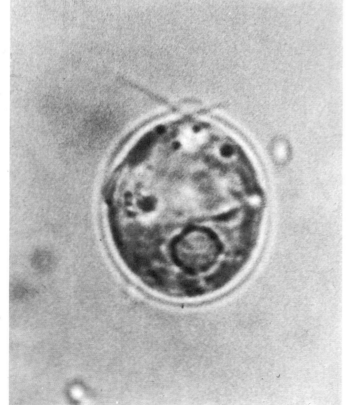

Algae

Fig. 1. High power studies of *Pleurococcus* and *Chlamydomonas*, CHLOROPHYCEAE

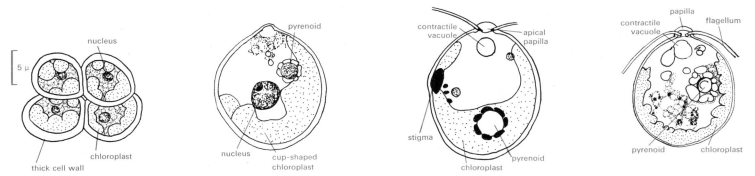

Pleurococcus—phase contrast   *Chlamydomonas*—fixed preparation   *Chlamydomonas*—living material, light microscope and phase contrast

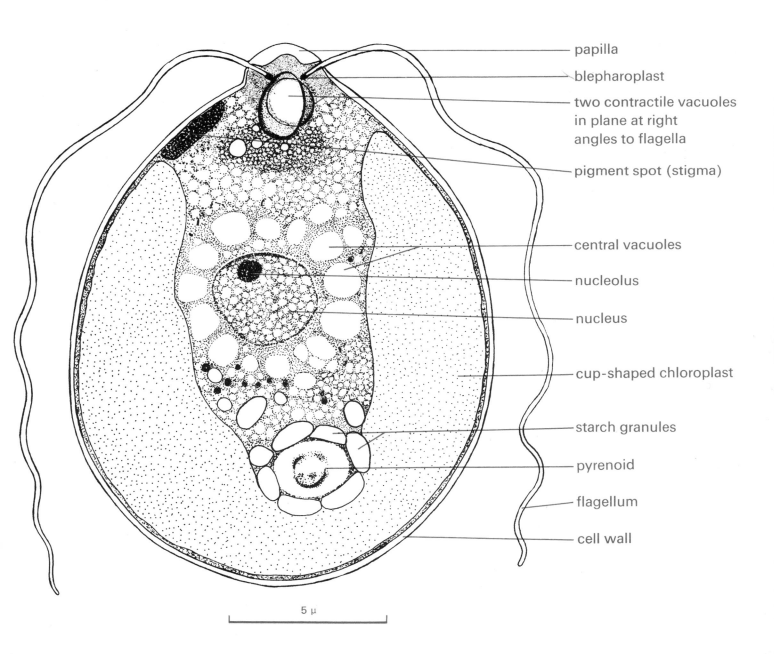

Composite drawing of *Chlamydomonas*

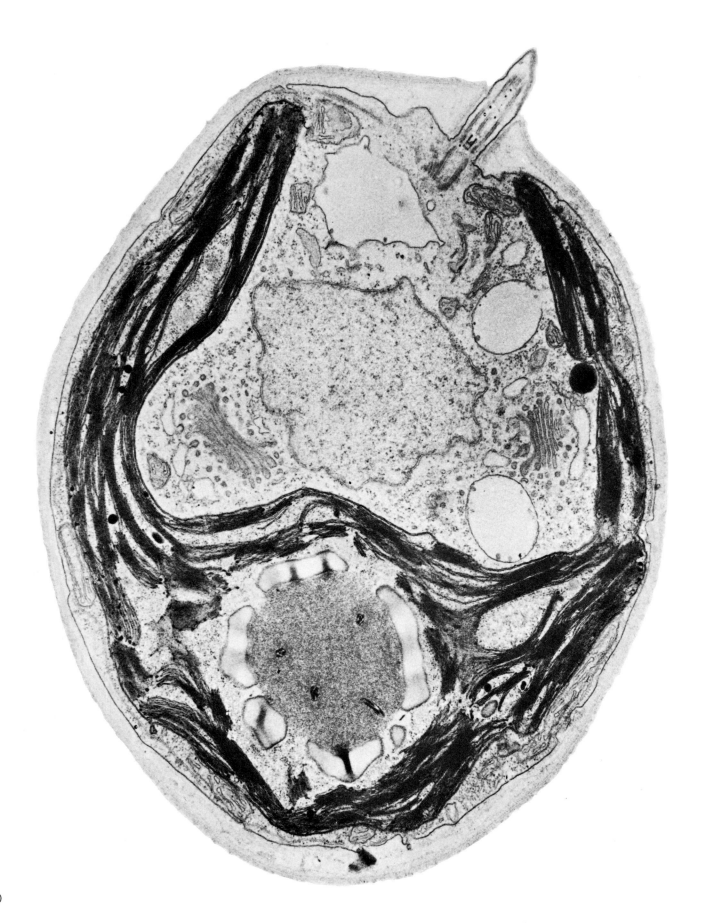

Fig. 2.   Section of *Chlamydomonas reinhardi* viewed under the electron microscope (by kind permission of G. E. Palade, the Rockefeller University, New York)

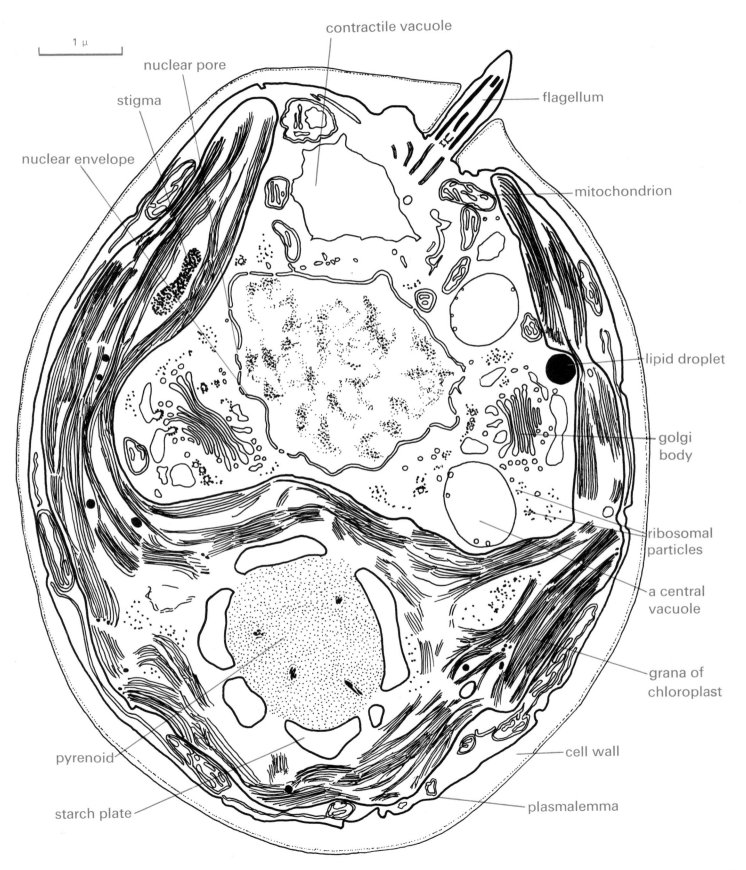

1 μ

contractile vacuole

nuclear pore

stigma

nuclear envelope

flagellum

mitochondrion

lipid droplet

golgi body

ribosomal particles

a central vacuole

grana of chloroplast

cell wall

plasmalemma

pyrenoid

starch plate

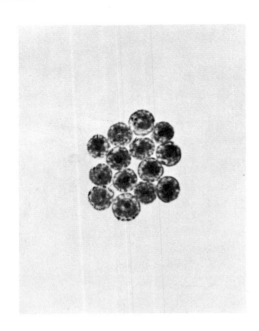
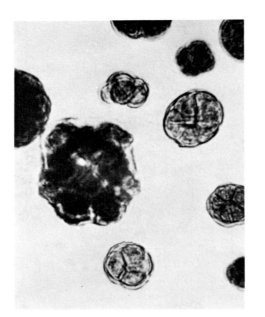
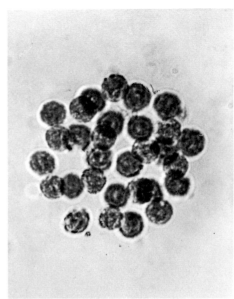
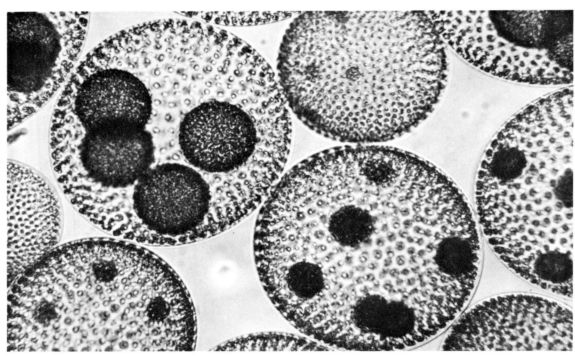
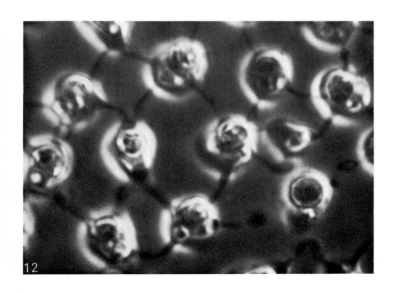
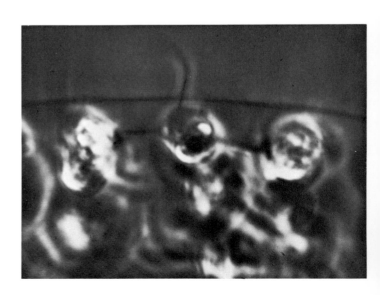

12

Fig. 3. High power studies of vegetative structure in Volvocales, CHLOROPHYCEAE

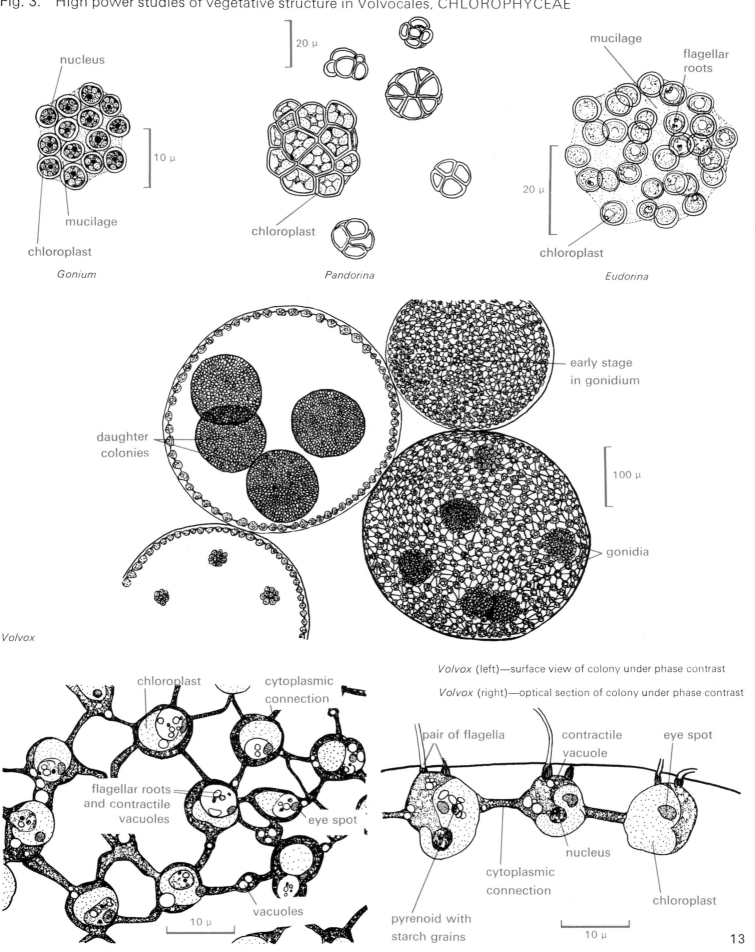

nucleus

mucilage

chloroplast

Gonium

10 μ

20 μ

chloroplast

Pandorina

mucilage

flagellar roots

20 μ

chloroplast

Eudorina

daughter colonies

early stage in gonidium

100 μ

gonidia

Volvox

chloroplast

cytoplasmic connection

flagellar roots and contractile vacuoles

eye spot

vacuoles

10 μ

Volvox (left)—surface view of colony under phase contrast

Volvox (right)—optical section of colony under phase contrast

pair of flagella

contractile vacuole

eye spot

nucleus

cytoplasmic connection

pyrenoid with starch grains

chloroplast

10 μ

13

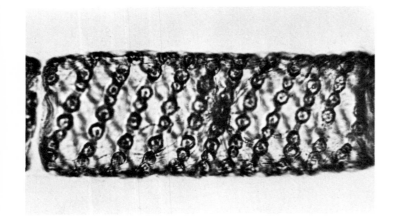
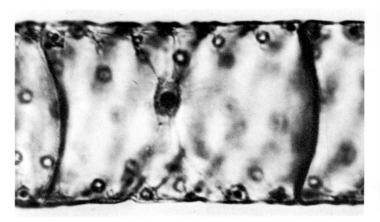
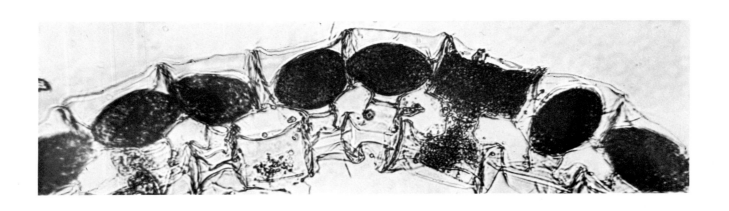
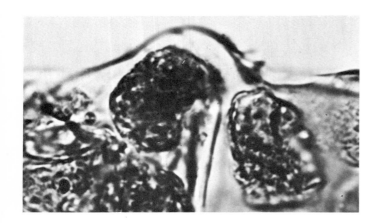
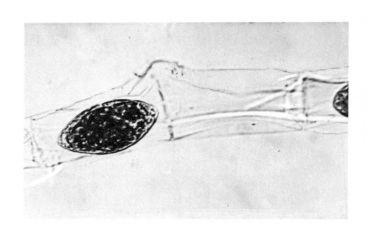
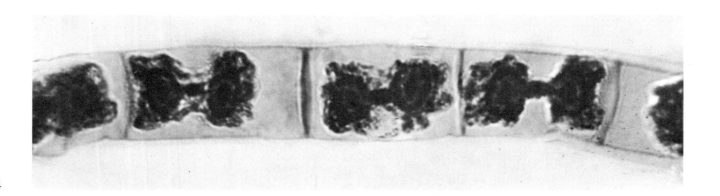

14

Fig. 4. High power studies of structure and reproduction in Conjugales, CHLOROPHYCEAE

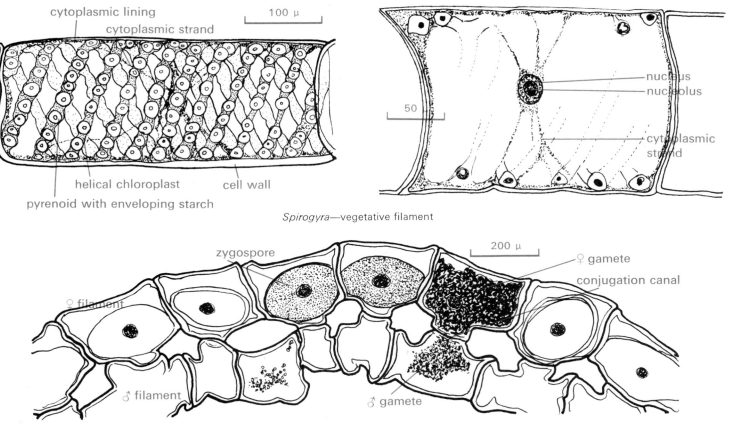

cytoplasmic lining
cytoplasmic strand
100 µ

helical chloroplast
cell wall
pyrenoid with enveloping starch

nucleus
nucleolus
50 µ
cytoplasmic strand

Spirogyra—vegetative filament

zygospore
200 µ
♀ gamete
conjugation canal
♀ filament
♂ filament
♂ gamete

Spirogyra—scalariform conjugation

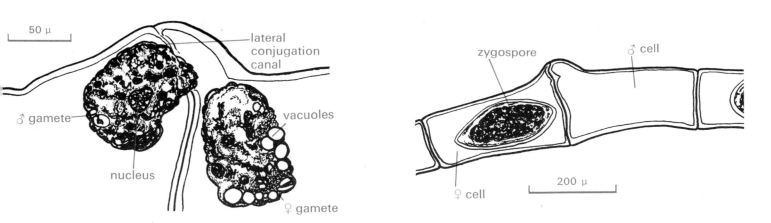

50 µ
lateral conjugation canal
♂ gamete
vacuoles
nucleus
♀ gamete

zygospore
♂ cell
♀ cell
200 µ

Spirogyra—lateral conjugation

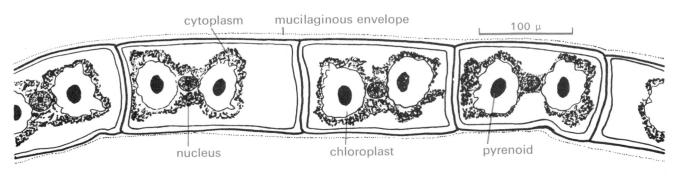

cytoplasm
mucilaginous envelope
100 µ

nucleus
chloroplast
pyrenoid

Zygnema—vegetative filament

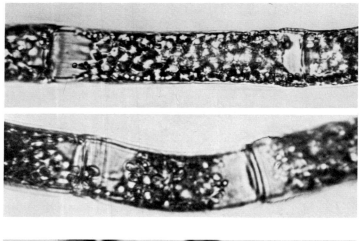

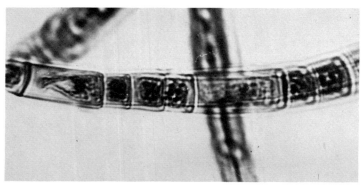

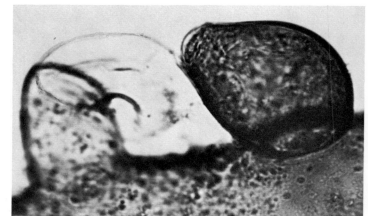

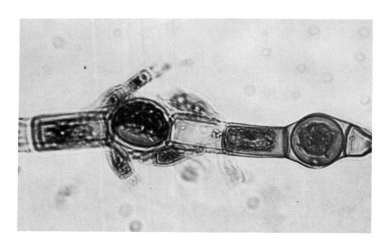

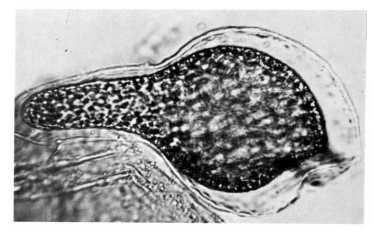

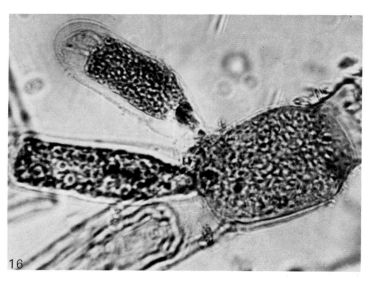

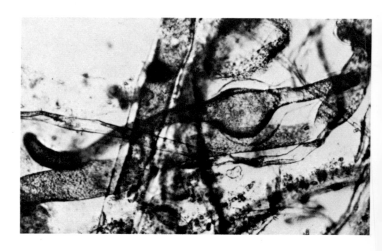

16

Fig. 5. High power studies of structure and reproduction in *Oedogonium*, CHLOROPHYCEAE

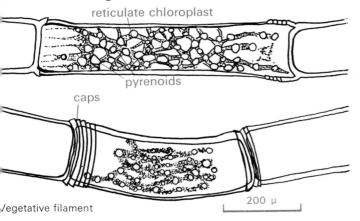

reticulate chloroplast

pyrenoids

caps

Vegetative filament

200 μ

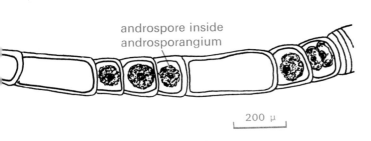

androspore inside androsporangium

200 μ

Androsporangia

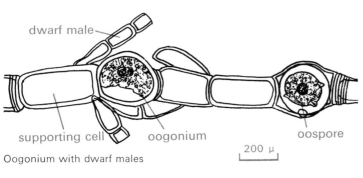

dwarf male

supporting cell   oogonium   oospore

Oogonium with dwarf males

200 μ

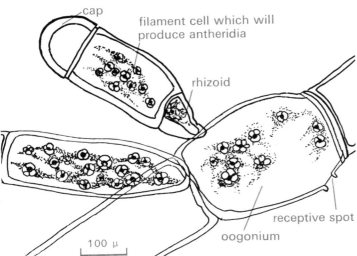

cap

filament cell which will produce antheridia

rhizoid

receptive spot

oogonium

100 μ

Details of dwarf male attached to oogonium

Fig. 6. High power studies of reproduction in *Vaucheria*, XANTHOPHYCEAE

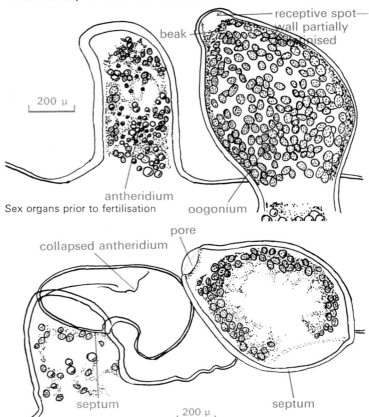

receptive spot

wall partially organised

beak

200 μ

antheridium

oogonium

Sex organs prior to fertilisation

pore

collapsed antheridium

septum

septum

200 μ

Sex organs after fertilisation

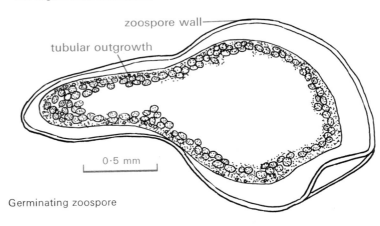

zoospore wall

tubular outgrowth

0·5 mm

Germinating zoospore

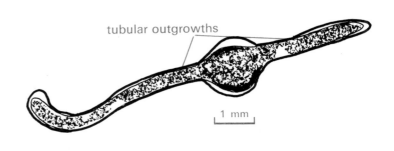

tubular outgrowths

1 mm

Germinating zoospore—later stage

17

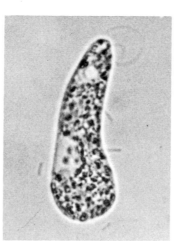
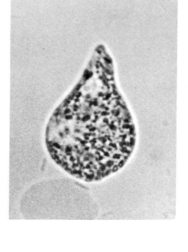
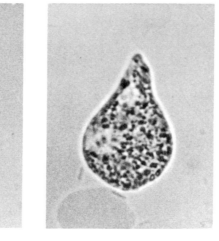

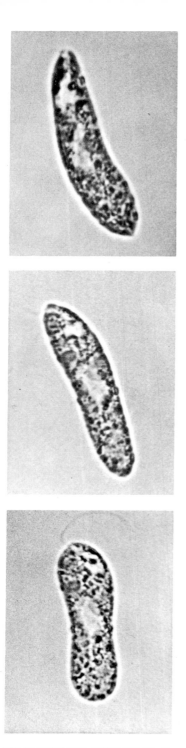
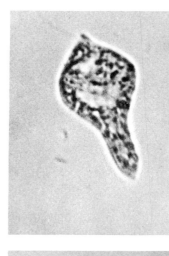

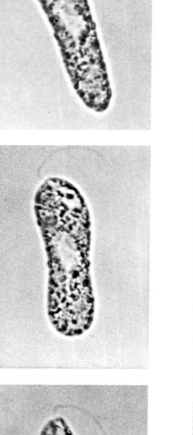

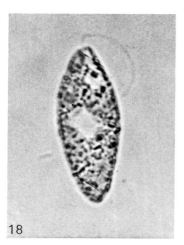
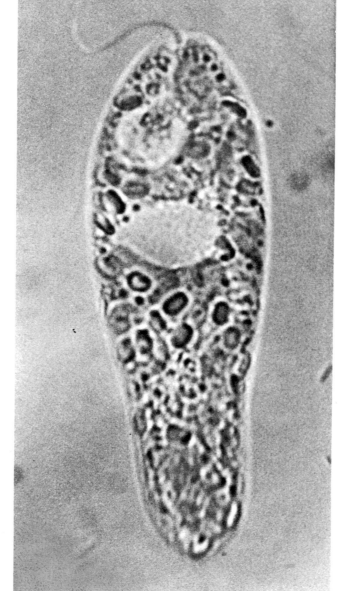
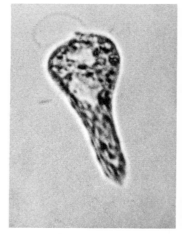

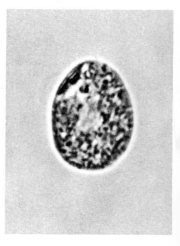

18

Fig. 7.   Light microscope studies of living *Euglena gracilis*, EUGLENOPHYCEAE

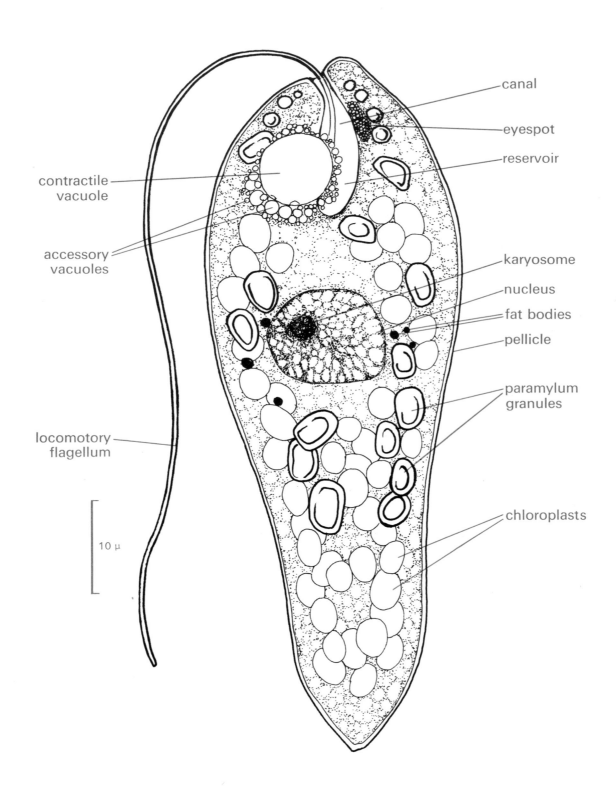

canal

eyespot

reservoir

contractile
vacuole

accessory
vacuoles

karyosome

nucleus

fat bodies

pellicle

paramylum
granules

locomotory
flagellum

chloroplasts

10 μ

A drawing of *Euglena gracilis* showing only those structures normally
visible with the aid of the light microscope
The small photographs arranged clockwise demonstrate euglenoid movement

19

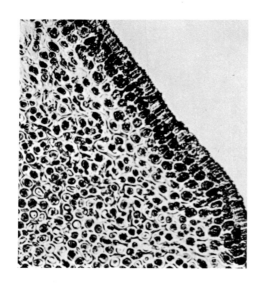
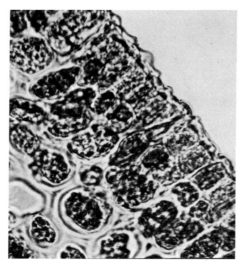
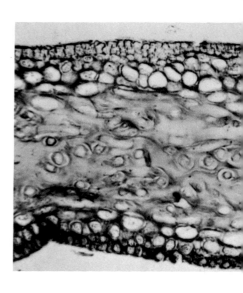

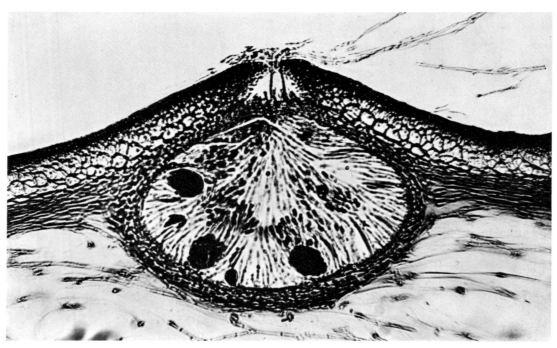

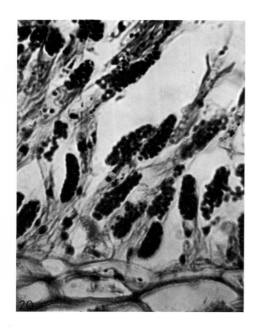
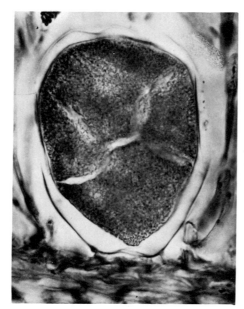
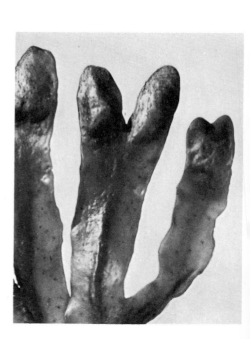

Fig. 8. Studies of the structure and reproduction of *Fucus*, PHAEOPHYCEAE

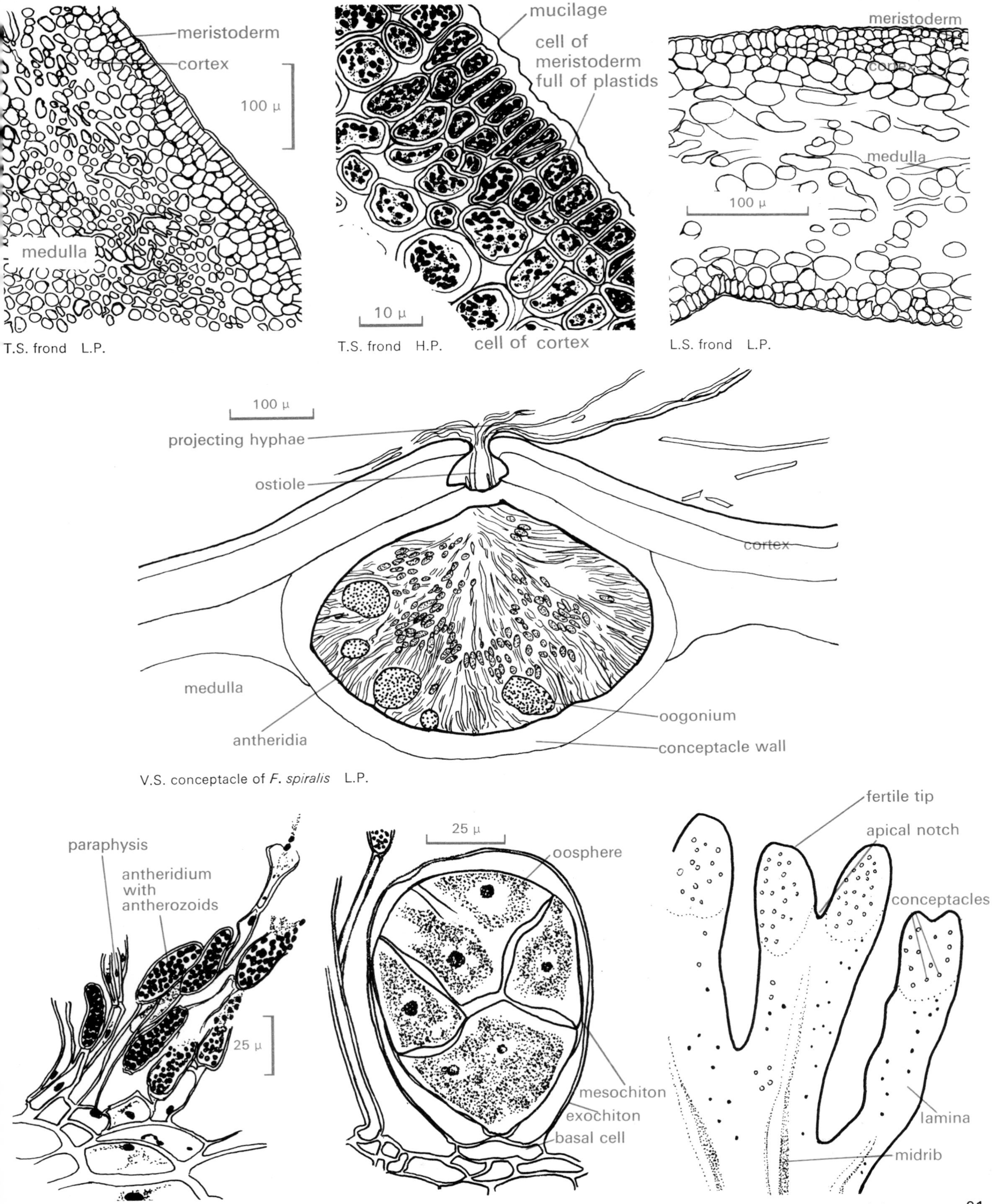

meristoderm
cortex

100 μ

medulla

T.S. frond   L.P.

mucilage
cell of
meristoderm
full of plastids

10 μ

cell of cortex

T.S. frond   H.P.

meristoderm
cortex

medulla

100 μ

L.S. frond   L.P.

100 μ

projecting hyphae

ostiole

cortex

medulla

antheridia

oogonium

conceptacle wall

V.S. conceptacle of *F. spiralis*   L.P.

paraphysis

antheridium
with
antherozoids

25 μ

Antheridia   H.P.

25 μ

oosphere

mesochiton
exochiton
basal cell

Oogonium   H.P.

fertile tip

apical notch

conceptacles

lamina

midrib

Portion of frond   L.P.—natural size

21

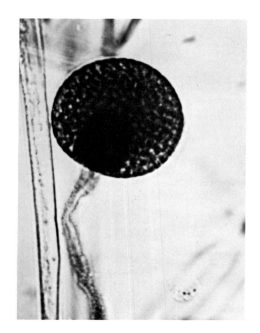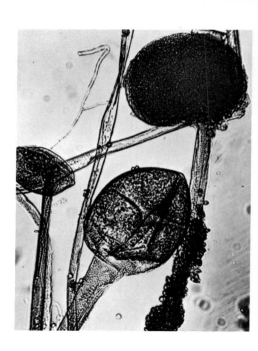

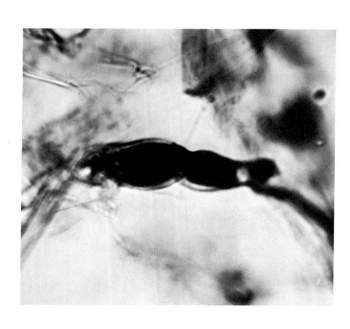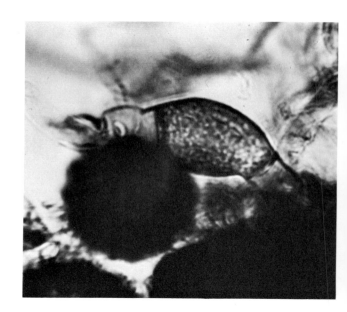

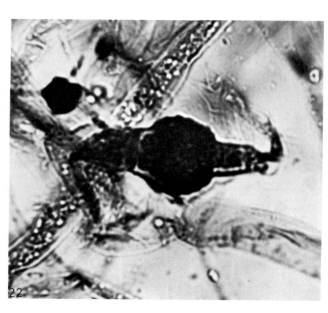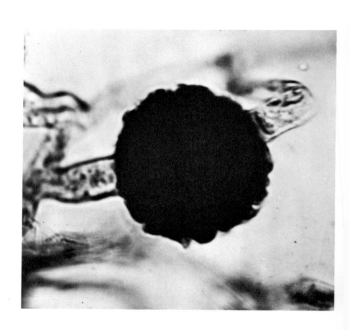

22

Fungi

Fig. 9. High power studies of asexual and sexual reproductive stages in *Mucor* and *Rhizopus*, PHYCOMYCETES

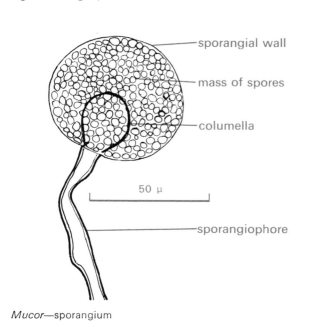

sporangial wall

mass of spores

columella

50 μ

sporangiophore

Mucor—sporangium

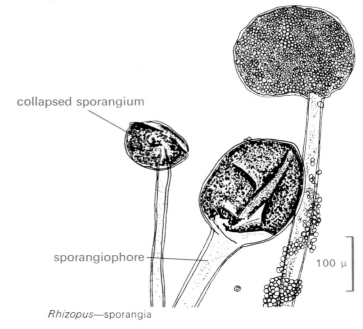

collapsed sporangium

sporangiophore

100 μ

Rhizopus—sporangia

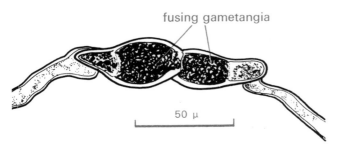

fusing gametangia

50 μ

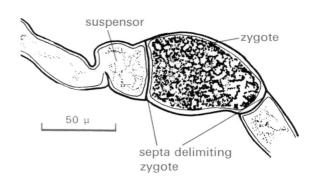

suspensor

zygote

50 μ

septa delimiting zygote

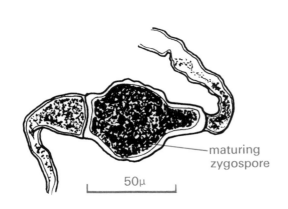

maturing zygospore

50μ

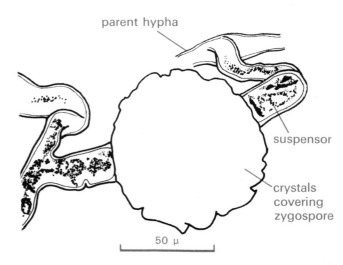

parent hypha

suspensor

crystals covering zygospore

50 μ

Mucor—stages in conjugation

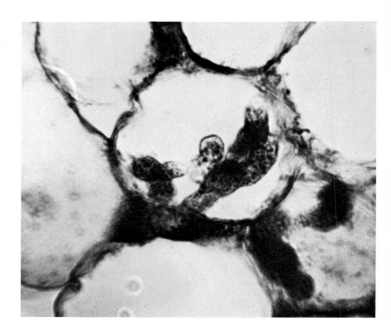

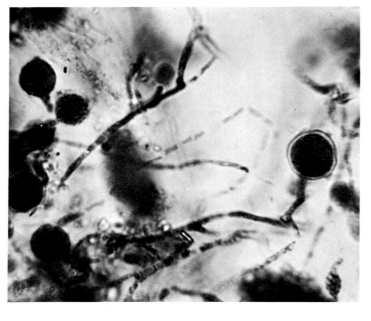

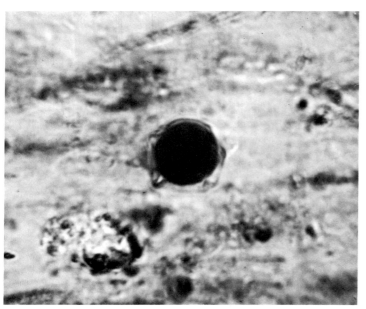

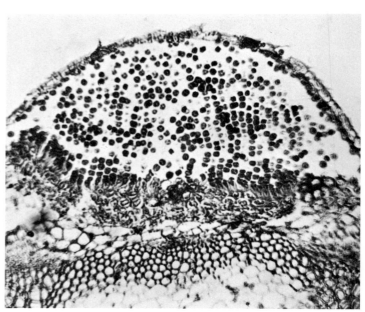

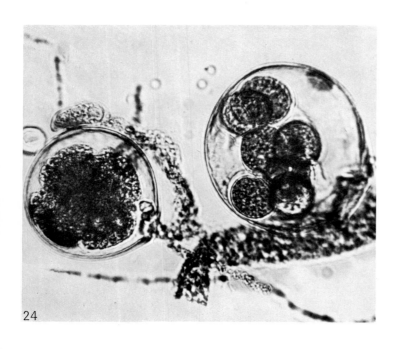

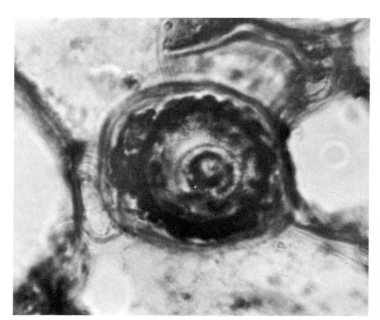

24

Fig. 10. High power studies of structure and reproduction in *Pythium*, *Peronospora*, *Cystopus*, and *Saprolegnia*, PHYCOMYCETES

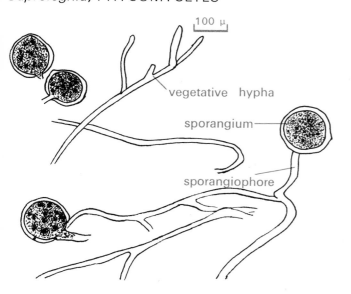

Pythium—sporangium

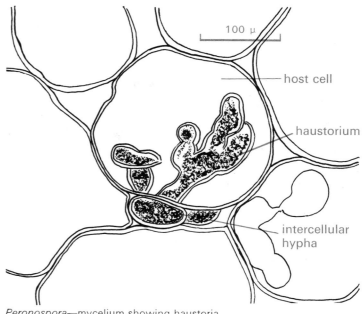

Peronospora—mycelium showing haustoria

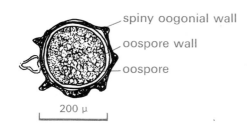

Pythium—oospore

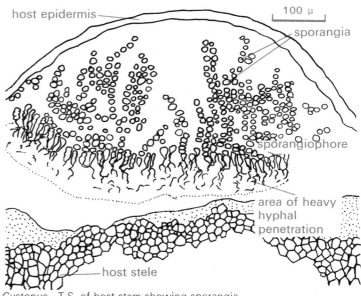

Cystopus—T.S. of host stem showing sporangia

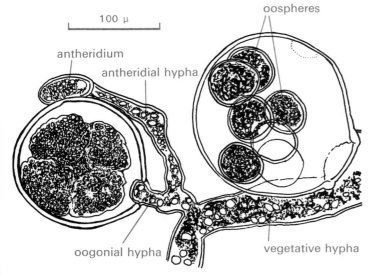

Saprolegnia—antheridium, oogonium and oospheres

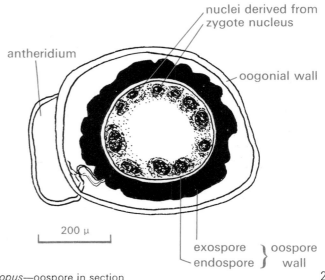

Cystopus—oospore in section

25

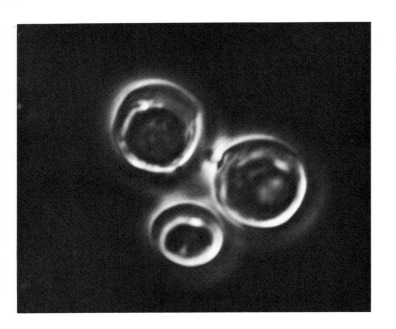

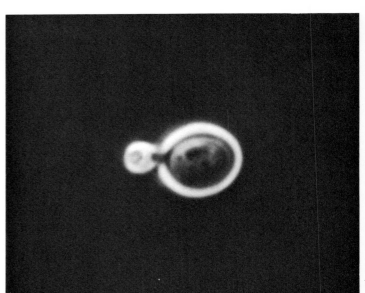

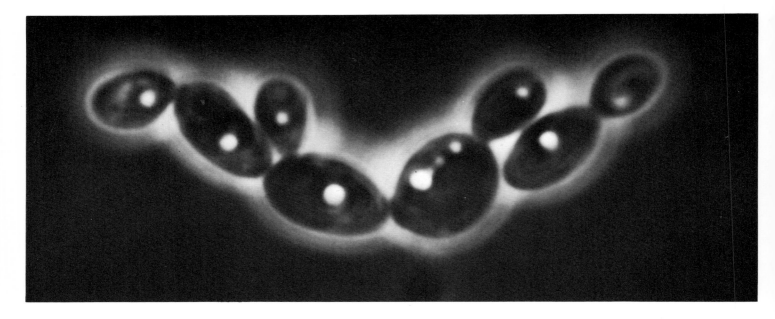

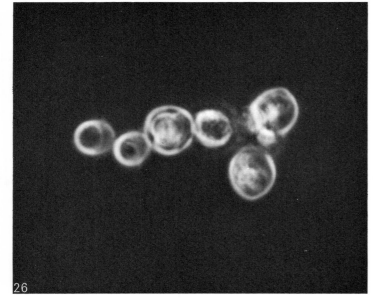

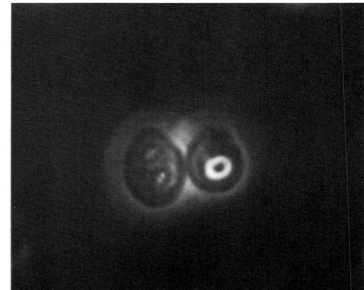

26

Fig. 11. Phase contrast studies of *Saccharomyces*, ASCOMYCETES

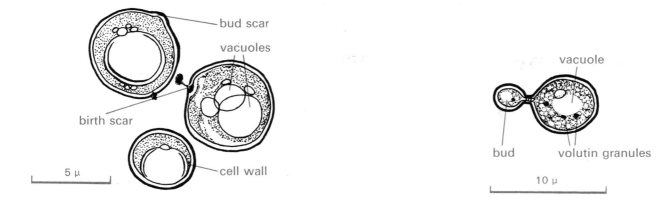

bud scar

vacuoles

birth scar

cell wall

5 μ

Vegetative cells

vacuole

bud

volutin granules

10 μ

Budding

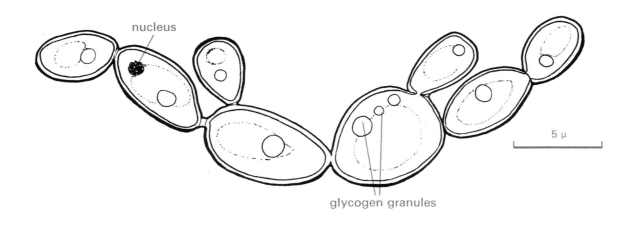

nucleus

glycogen granules

5 μ

Pseudomycelium

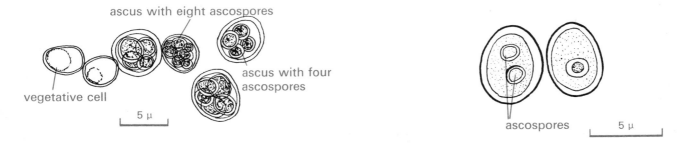

ascus with eight ascospores

ascus with four
ascospores

vegetative cell

5 μ

ascospores

5 μ

Asci

27

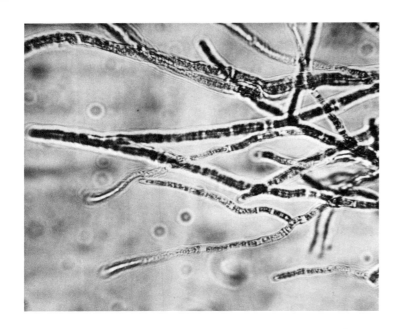

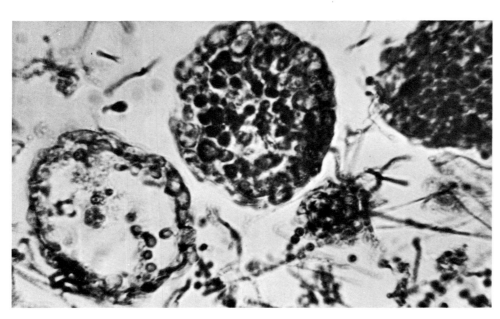
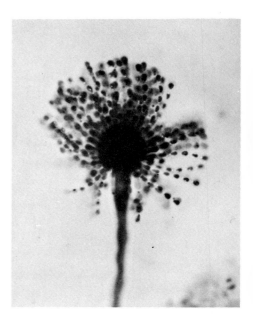
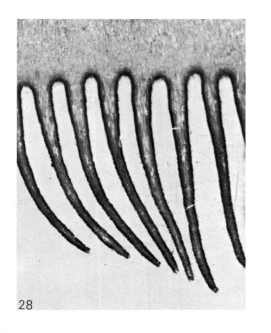
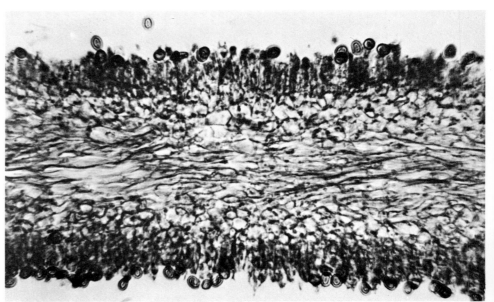

28

Fig. 12.   High Power studies of *Aspergillus* (*Eurotium*), ASCOMYCETES

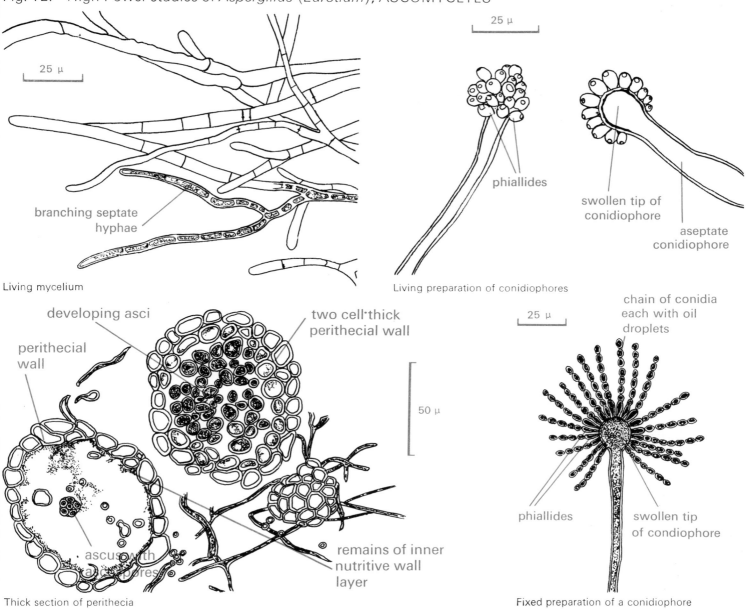

25 μ

25 μ

phiallides

swollen tip of
conidiophore

aseptate
conidiophore

branching septate
hyphae

Living mycelium

Living preparation of conidiophores

developing asci

two cell thick
perithecial wall

perithecial
wall

50 μ

25 μ

chain of conidia
each with oil
droplets

ascus with
ascospores

remains of inner
nutritive wall
layer

phiallides

swollen tip
of condiophore

Thick section of perithecia

Fixed preparation of a conidiophore

Fig. 13.   Studies of a section through the pileus of *Psalliota hortensis*, BASIDIOMYCETES

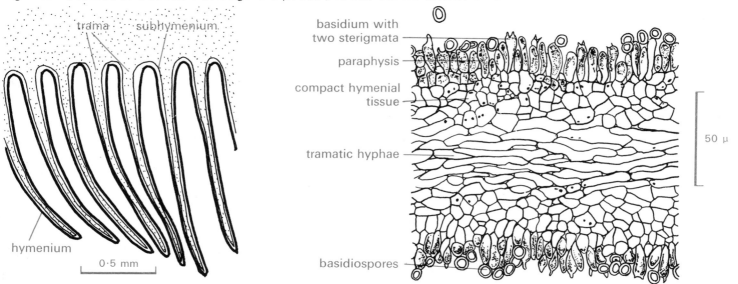

trama   subhymenium

basidium with
two sterigmata

paraphysis

compact hymenial
tissue

tramatic hyphae

50 μ

hymenium

0·5 mm

basidiospores

Vertical section   L.P.

V.S. portion of a gill   H.P.

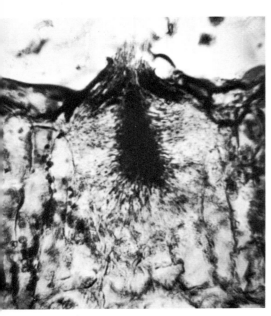
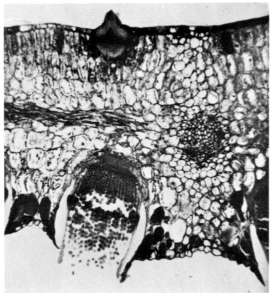
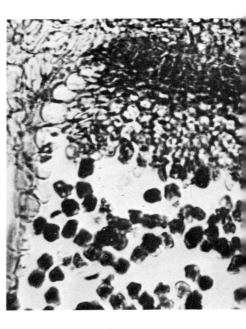
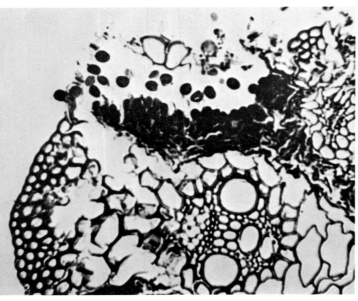
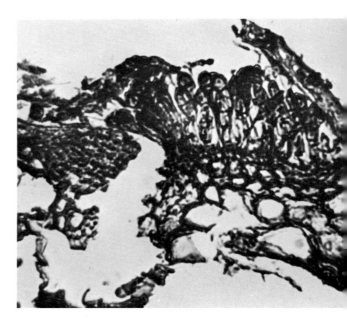
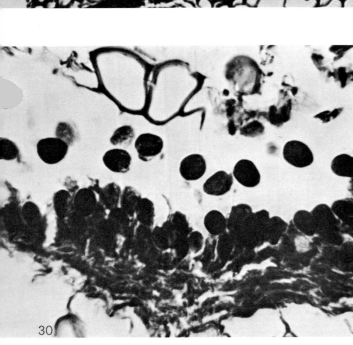
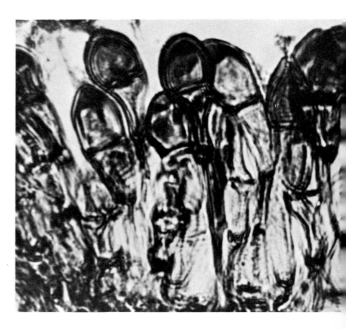

30

Fig. 14. Sporulating stages of *Puccinia graminis*, BASIDIOMYCETES

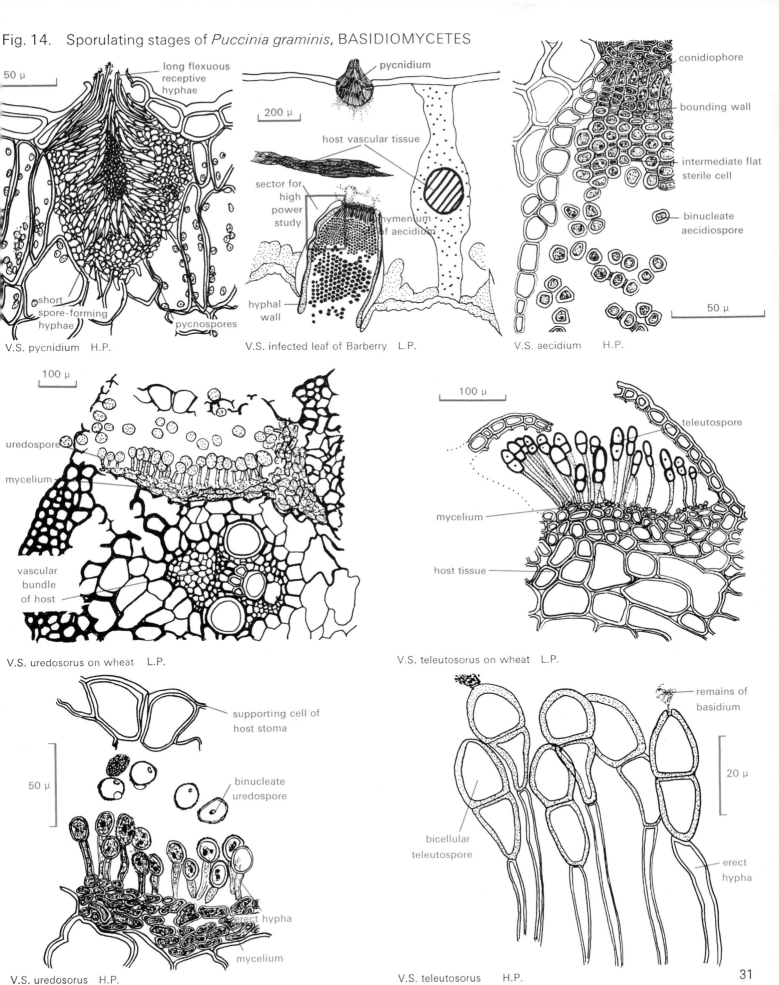

50 µ

long flexuous
receptive
hyphae

short
spore-forming
hyphae

pycnospores

V.S. pycnidium   H.P.

pycnidium

200 µ

host vascular tissue

sector for
high
power
study

hymenium
of aecidium

hyphal
wall

V.S. infected leaf of Barberry   L.P.

conidiophore

bounding wall

intermediate flat
sterile cell

binucleate
aecidiospore

50 µ

V.S. aecidium   H.P.

100 µ

uredospore

mycelium

vascular
bundle
of host

V.S. uredosorus on wheat   L.P.

100 µ

teleutospore

mycelium

host tissue

V.S. teleutosorus on wheat   L.P.

supporting cell of
host stoma

binucleate
uredospore

50 µ

erect hypha

mycelium

V.S. uredosorus   H.P.

remains of
basidium

20 µ

bicellular
teleutospore

erect
hypha

V.S. teleutosorus   H.P.

31

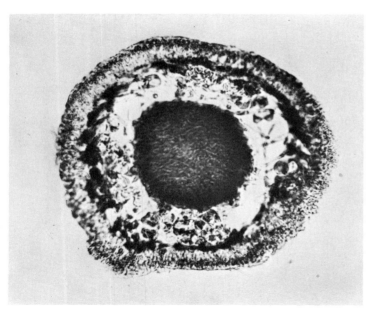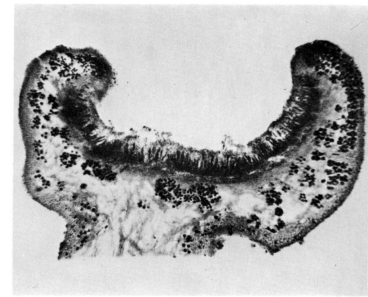

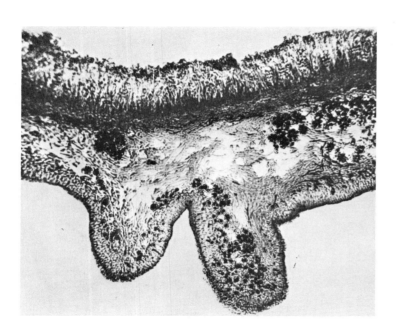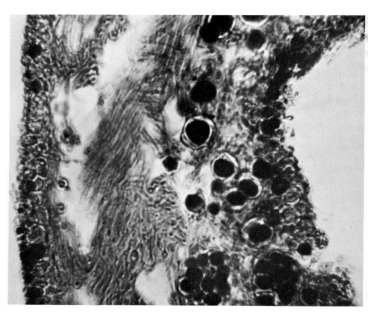

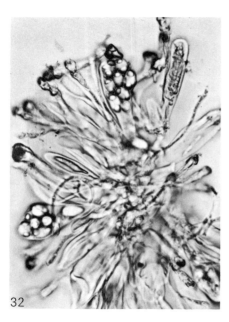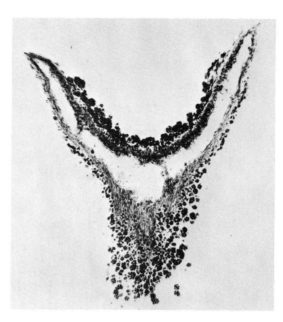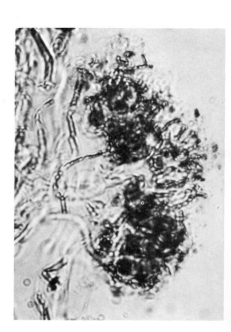

Lichenes

Fig. 15. Studies of ascomycete lichens

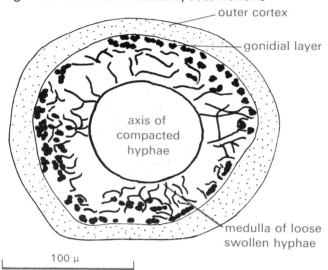

T.S. thallus of a fruticose lichen, *Usnea*   L.P.

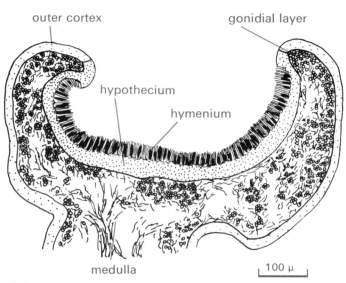

V.S. apothecium of a foliose lichen, *Parmelia* (*Hypogymnia*)   L.P.

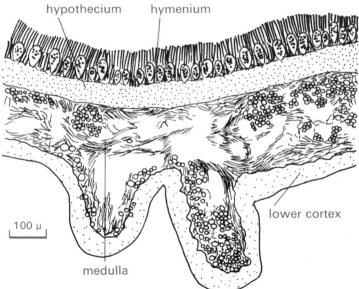

V.S. apothecium of a foliose lichen, *Xanthoria*   L.P.

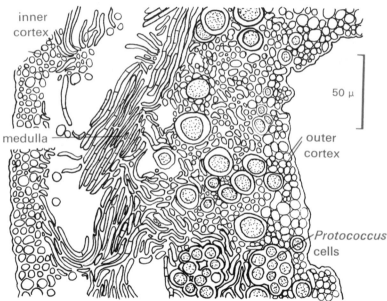

T.S. thallus of *Parmelia*   H.P.

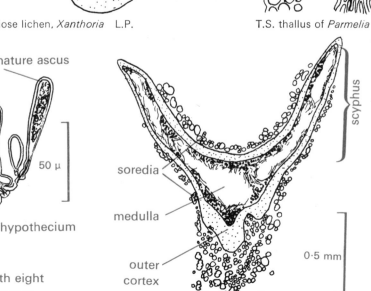

Macerated hymenium of *Xanthoria*   H.P.   V.S. podetium of *Cladonia*   L.P.

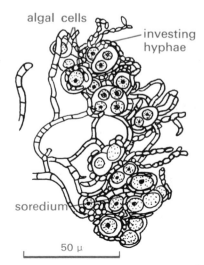

Soredia of *Cladonia*   H.P.

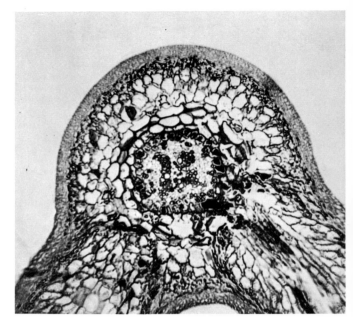

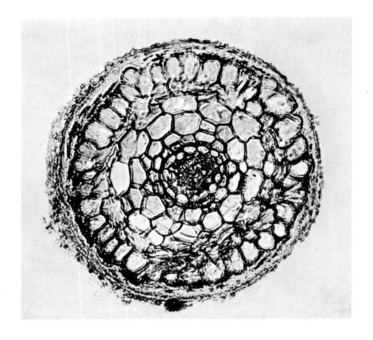

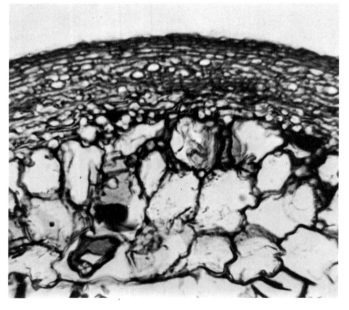

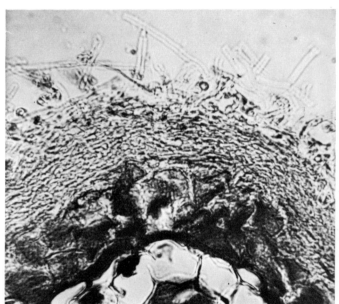

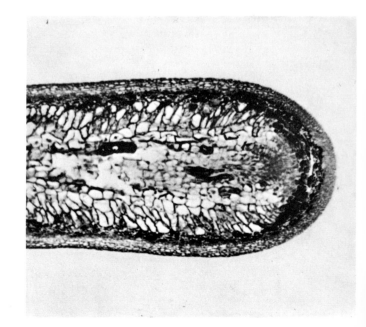

34

Mycorrhiza

Fig. 16. Studies of the ectotrophic mycorrhiza of the root of *Fagus sylvatica*, the Beech

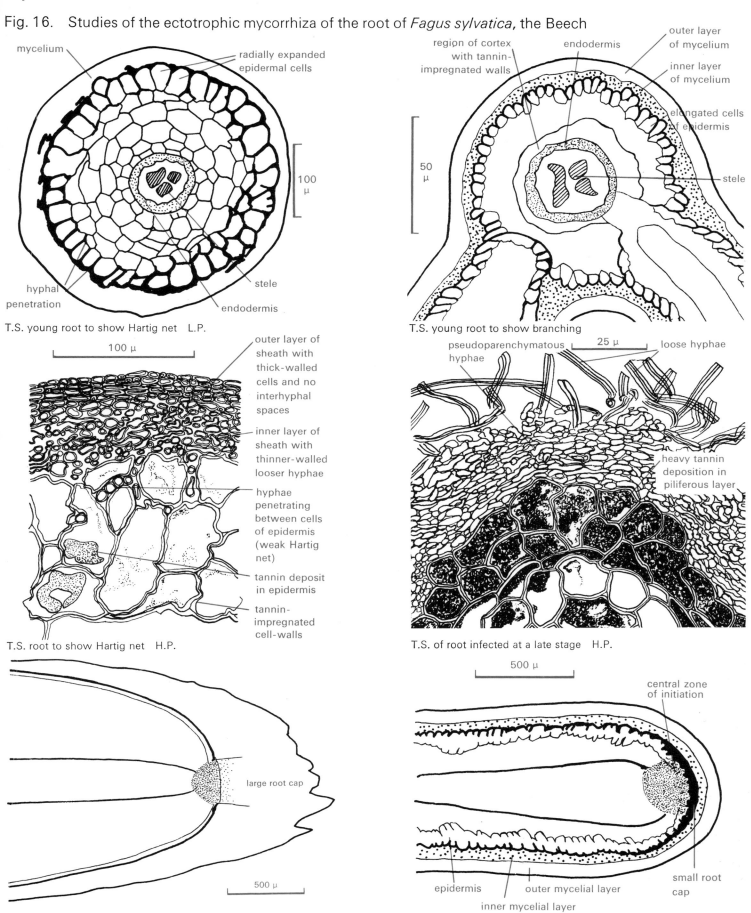

T.S. young root to show Hartig net   L.P.

T.S. young root to show branching

T.S. root to show Hartig net   H.P.

T.S. of root infected at a late stage   H.P.

L.S. uninfected root apex   L.P.

Glancing L.S. infected root apex   L.P.

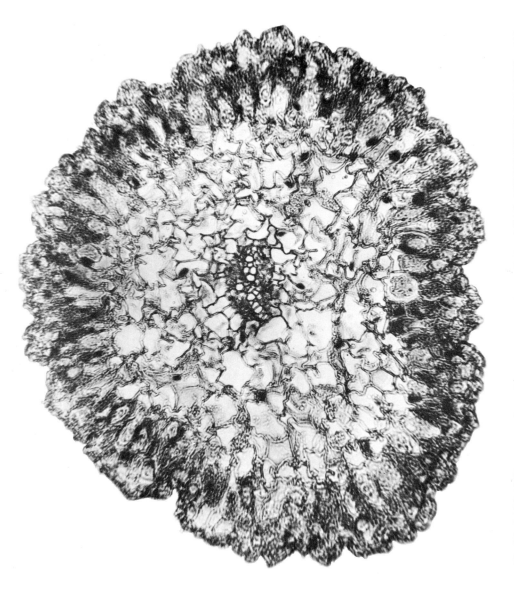

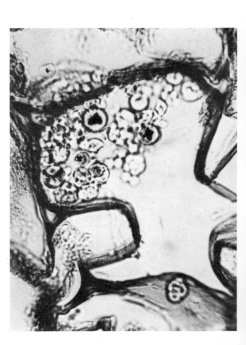

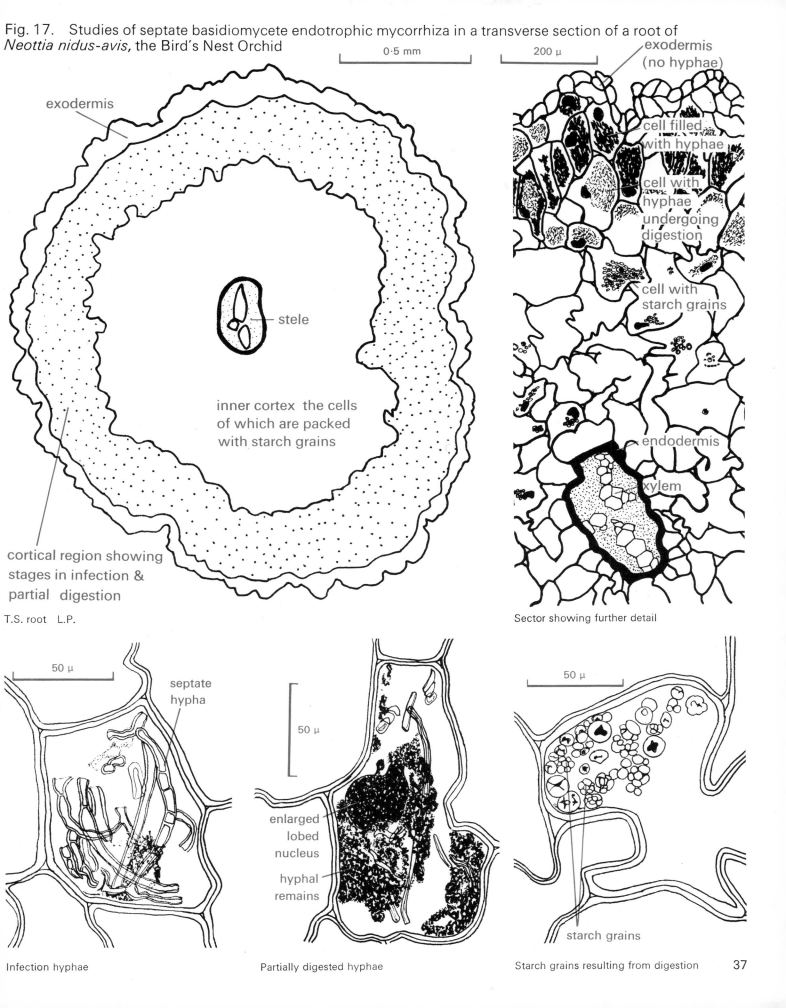

Fig. 17. Studies of septate basidiomycete endotrophic mycorrhiza in a transverse section of a root of *Neottia nidus-avis*, the Bird's Nest Orchid

0·5 mm

200 μ

exodermis (no hyphae)

exodermis

cell filled with hyphae

cell with hyphae undergoing digestion

stele

cell with starch grains

inner cortex the cells of which are packed with starch grains

endodermis

xylem

cortical region showing stages in infection & partial digestion

T.S. root L.P.

Sector showing further detail

50 μ

septate hypha

50 μ

enlarged lobed nucleus

hyphal remains

50 μ

starch grains

Infection hyphae

Partially digested hyphae

Starch grains resulting from digestion

37

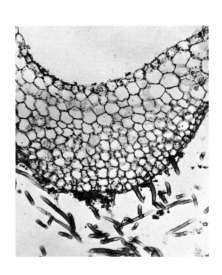

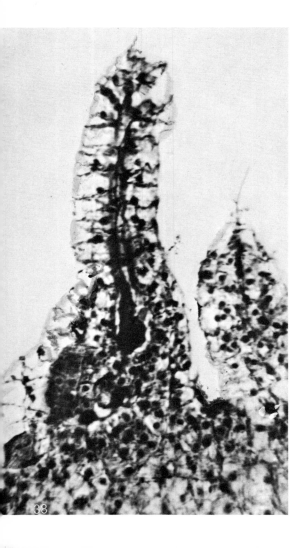

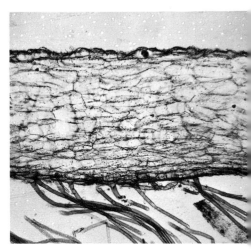

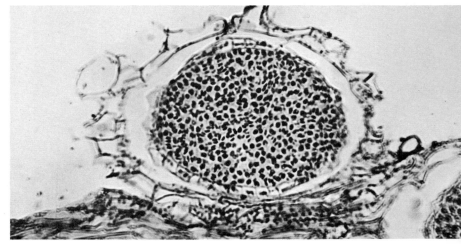

Bryophyta-Hepaticae

Fig. 18.   Life studies of *Pellia epiphylla*, METZGERIALES

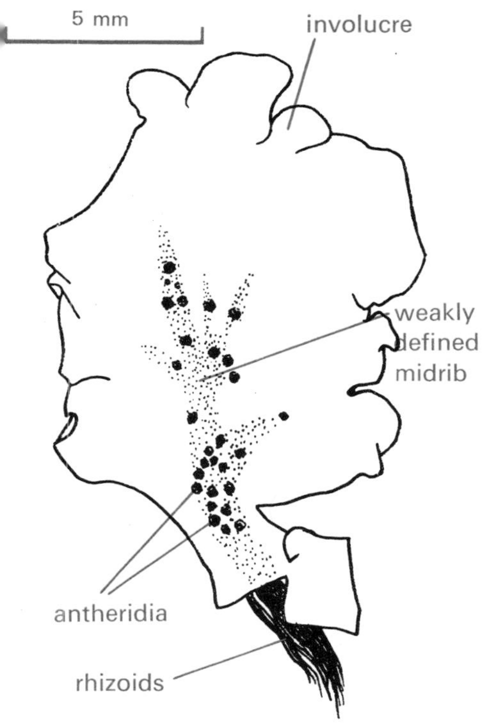

5 mm — involucre

weakly
defined
midrib

antheridia

rhizoids

Thallus bearing antheridia

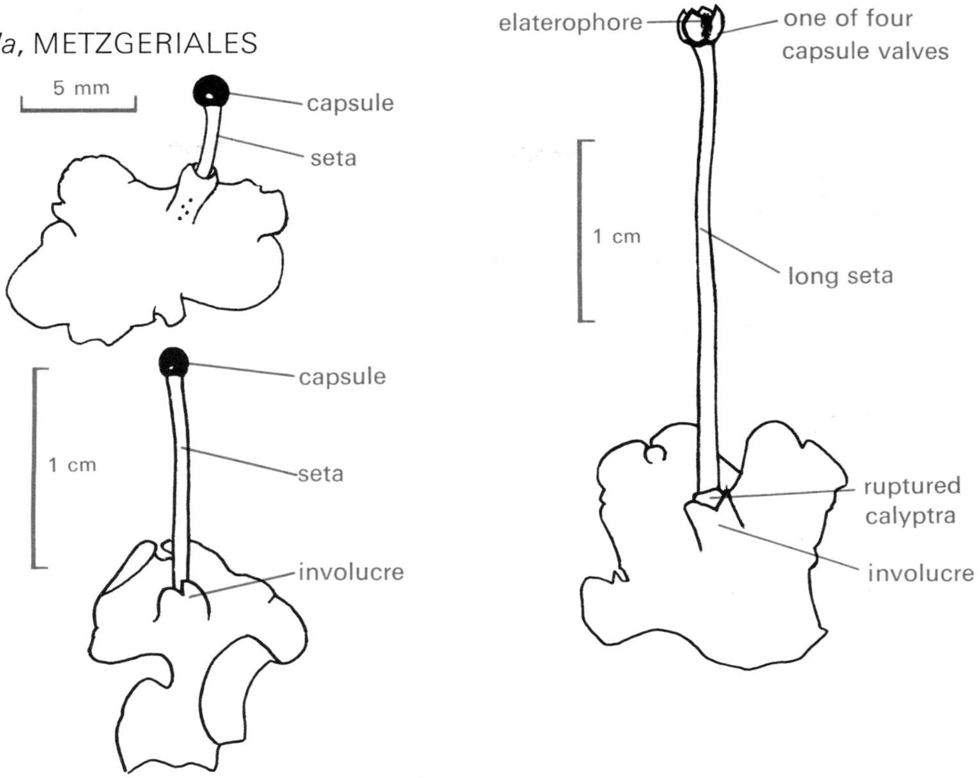

5 mm

capsule
seta

1 cm

capsule

seta

involucre

Stages in development of sporogonium

elaterophore — one of four
capsule valves

1 cm

long seta

ruptured
calyptra

involucre

Fig. 19.   Sections of gametophyte of *Pellia epiphylla*

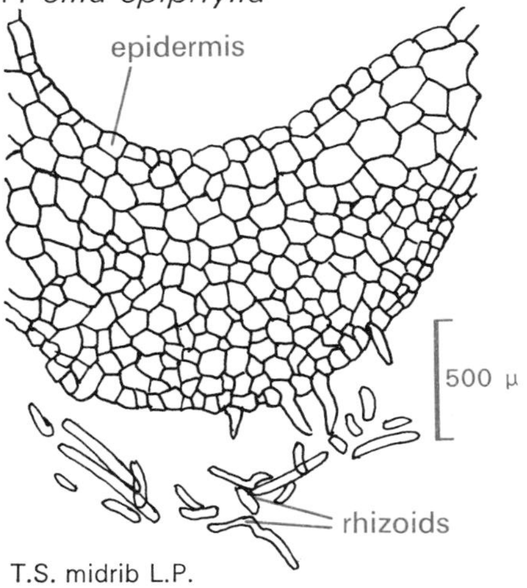

neck cell

25 μ

remains of
neck canal
cells

venter
canal cell

ovum

several
cell thick
venter wall

V.S. archegonium   H.P.

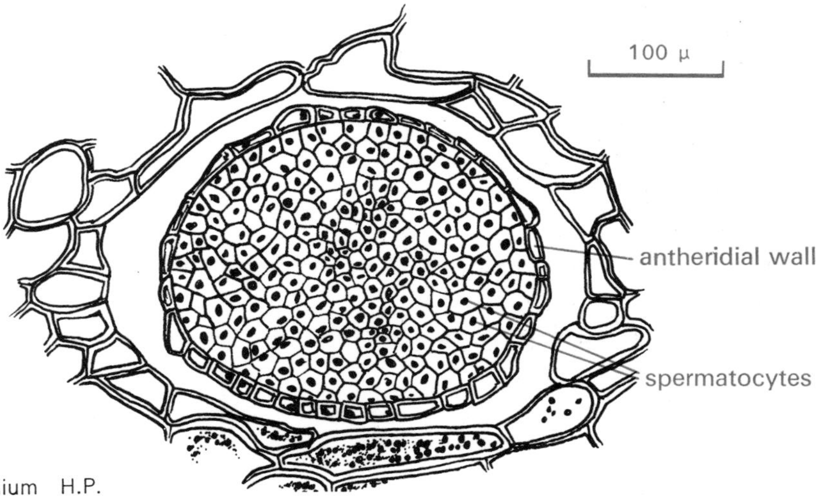

epidermis

500 μ

rhizoids

T.S. midrib L.P.

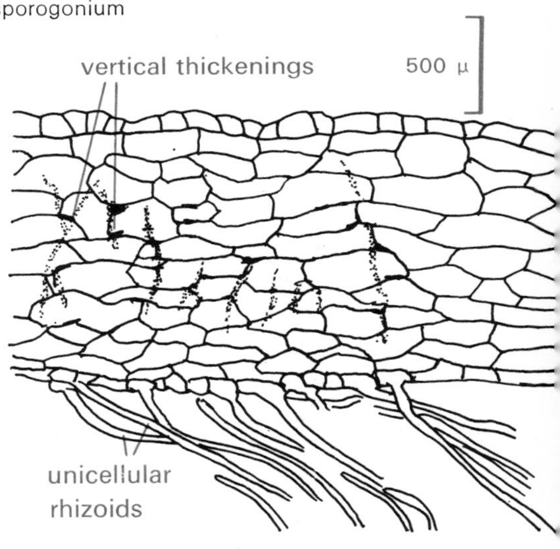

vertical thickenings

500 μ

unicellular
rhizoids

L.S. midrib   L.P.

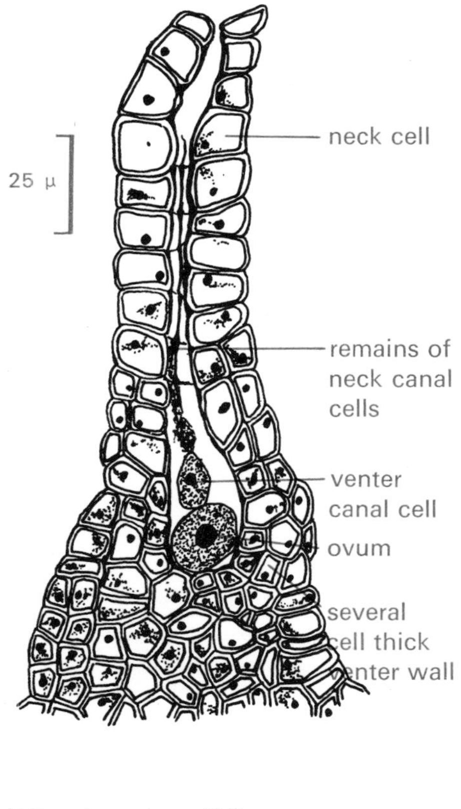

100 μ

antheridial wall

spermatocytes

V.S. antheridium   H.P.

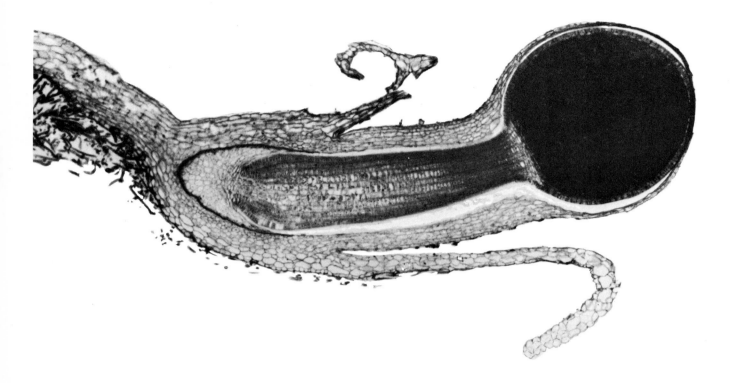

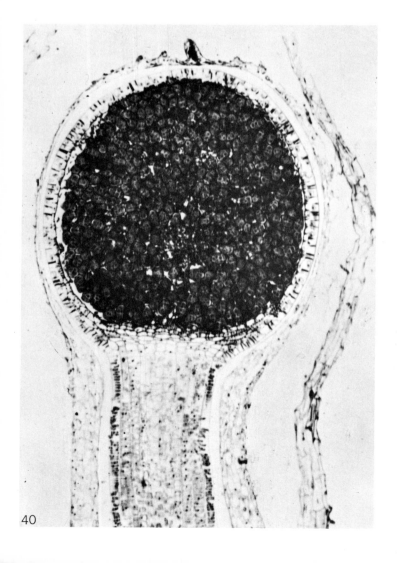

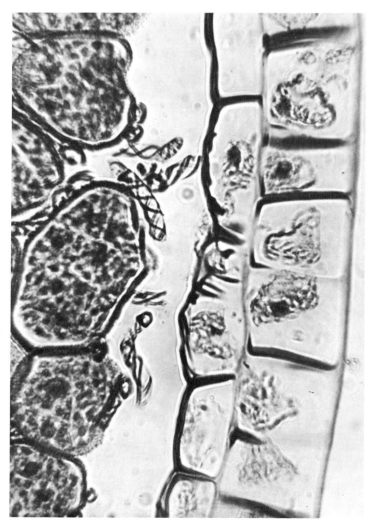

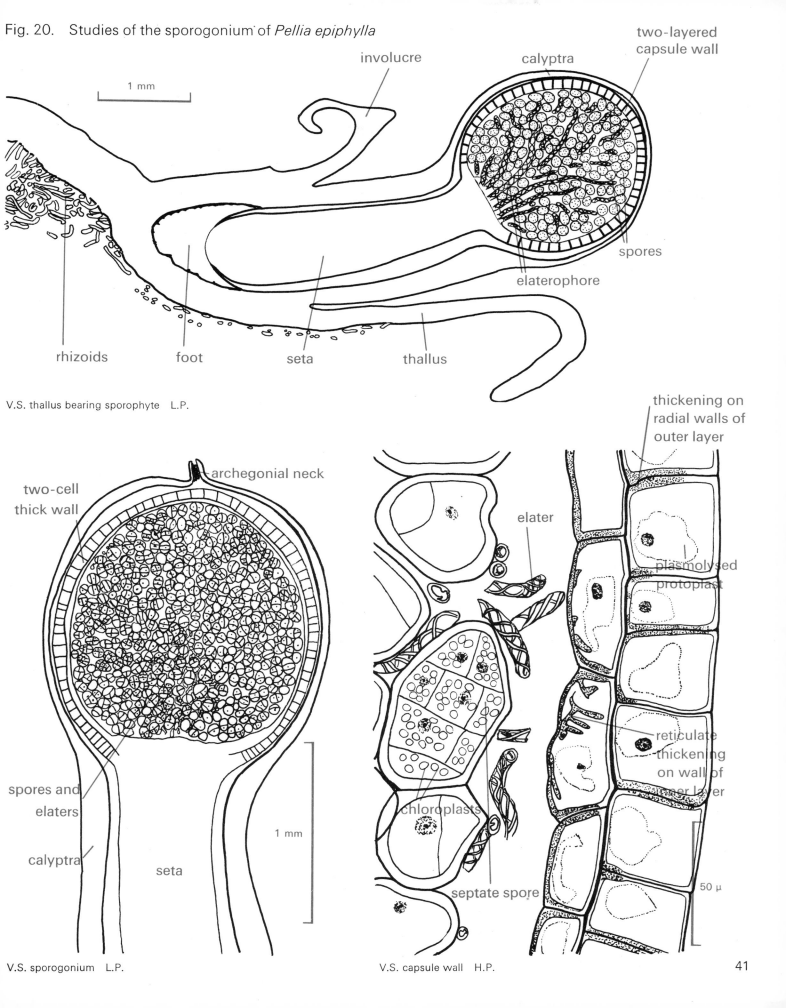

Fig. 20. Studies of the sporogonium of *Pellia epiphylla*

1 mm

involucre

calyptra

two-layered capsule wall

spores

elaterophore

rhizoids

foot

seta

thallus

V.S. thallus bearing sporophyte   L.P.

archegonial neck

two-cell thick wall

spores and elaters

calyptra

seta

1 mm

V.S. sporogonium   L.P.

thickening on radial walls of outer layer

elater

plasmolysed protoplast

reticulate thickening on wall of inner layer

chloroplasts

septate spore

50 μ

V.S. capsule wall   H.P.

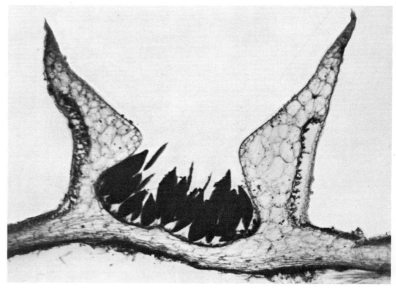

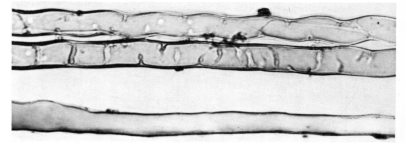

42

Fig. 21. Life studies of *Marchantia polymorpha*, MARCHANTIALES

Male plants

(life size)

antheridiophore

midrib

rhizoids

(life size)

Female plant

stalk

young archegoniophore

midrib

old gemmae cups

Antheridiophore—upper side

one of eight lobes

2 mm

antheridia

hyaline web

Archegoniophore—lower side

one of nine lobes

2 mm

developing sporogonium

groove containing rhizoids

Archegoniophore with mature sporogonia

seta

2 mm

dehisced sporogonium

stalk

Plant with gemmae cups

apical notch

cup

detail of marchantialian epidermis

gemmae

1 cm

V.S. gemma cup

0·5 mm

stalk

inner ledge

gemma

pore

septa

tubercles

20 μ

smooth wall

Tuberculate and smooth-walled rhizoids

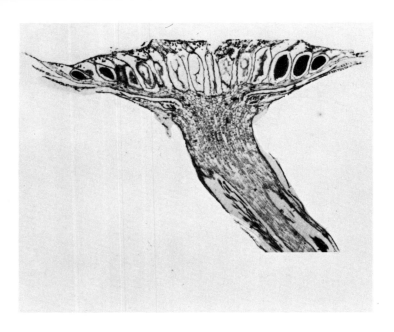
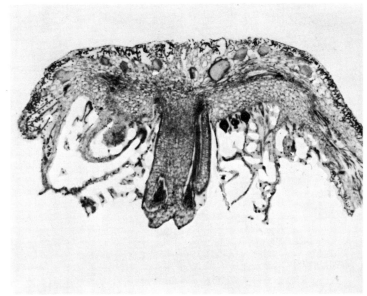
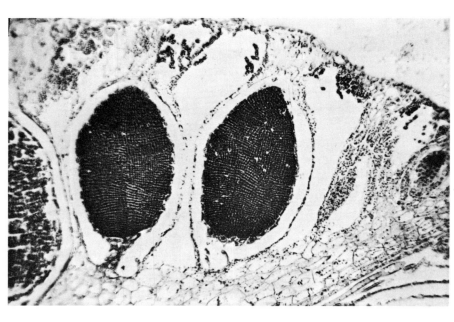

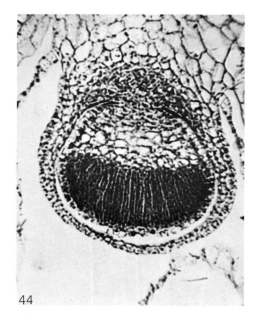
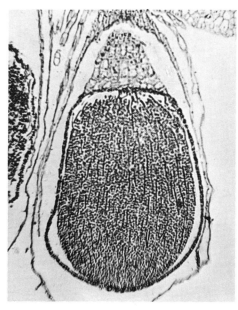
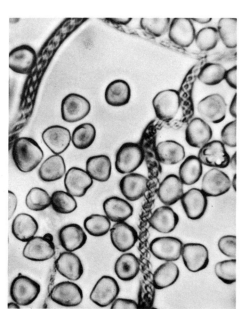

Fig. 22.   Studies of sexual reproduction in *Marchantia polymorpha*

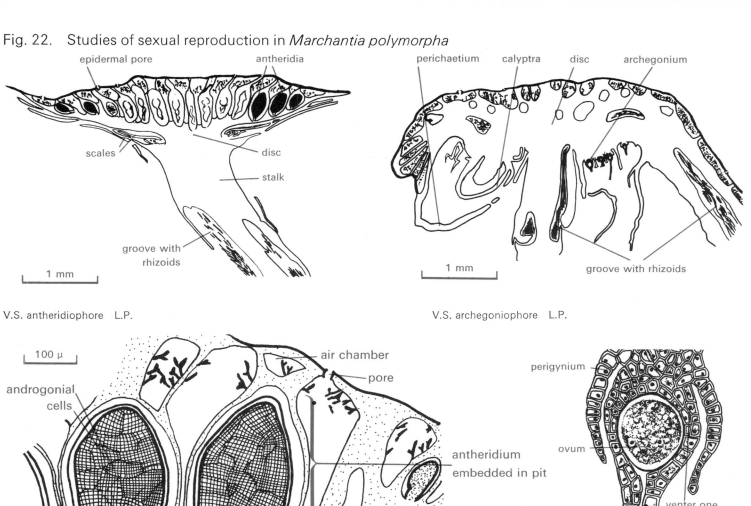

epidermal pore   antheridia   perichaetium   calyptra   disc   archegonium

scales   disc

stalk

groove with rhizoids

1 mm

groove with rhizoids

1 mm

V.S. antheridiophore   L.P.

V.S. archegoniophore   L.P.

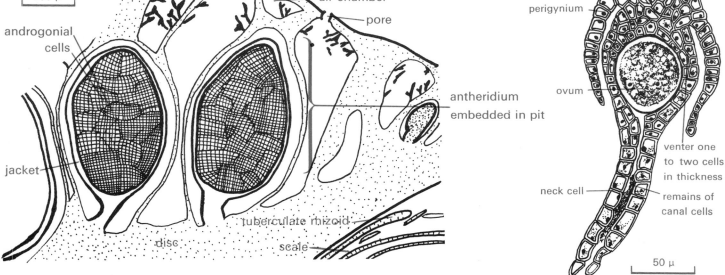

100 μ

air chamber

pore

androgonial cells

antheridium embedded in pit

jacket

tuberculate rhizoid

disc

scale

V.S. antheridiophore   H.P.

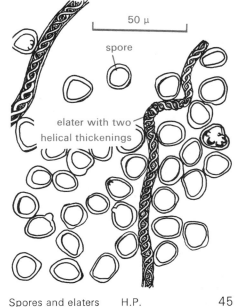

perigynium

ovum

venter one to two cells in thickness

neck cell

remains of canal cells

50 μ

V.S. archegonium   H.P.

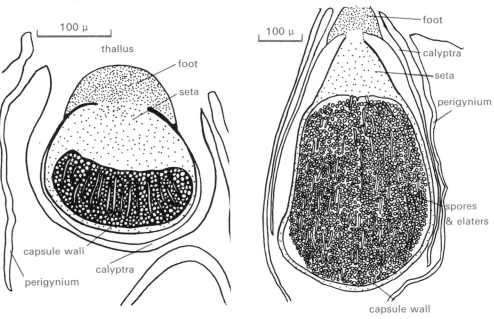

100 μ

thallus

foot

seta

100 μ

foot

calyptra

seta

perigynium

spores & elaters

capsule wall

calyptra

perigynium

capsule wall

V.S. young sporogonium   L.P.

V.S. sporogonium at a later stage   L.P.

50 μ

spore

elater with two helical thickenings

Spores and elaters   H.P.

45

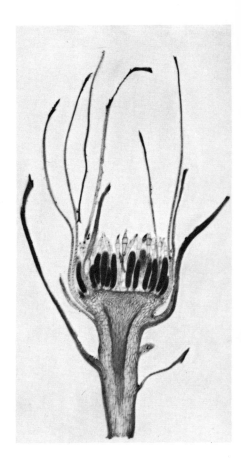

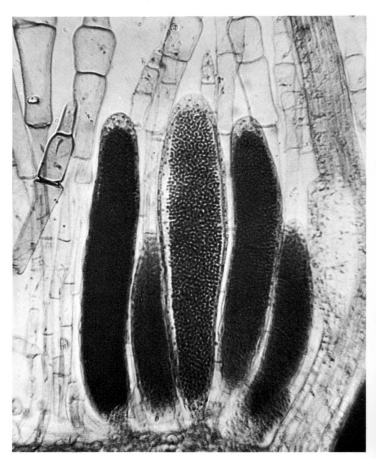

Fig. 23. Studies of the sexual reproductive organs of *Funaria hygrometrica*, BRYALES

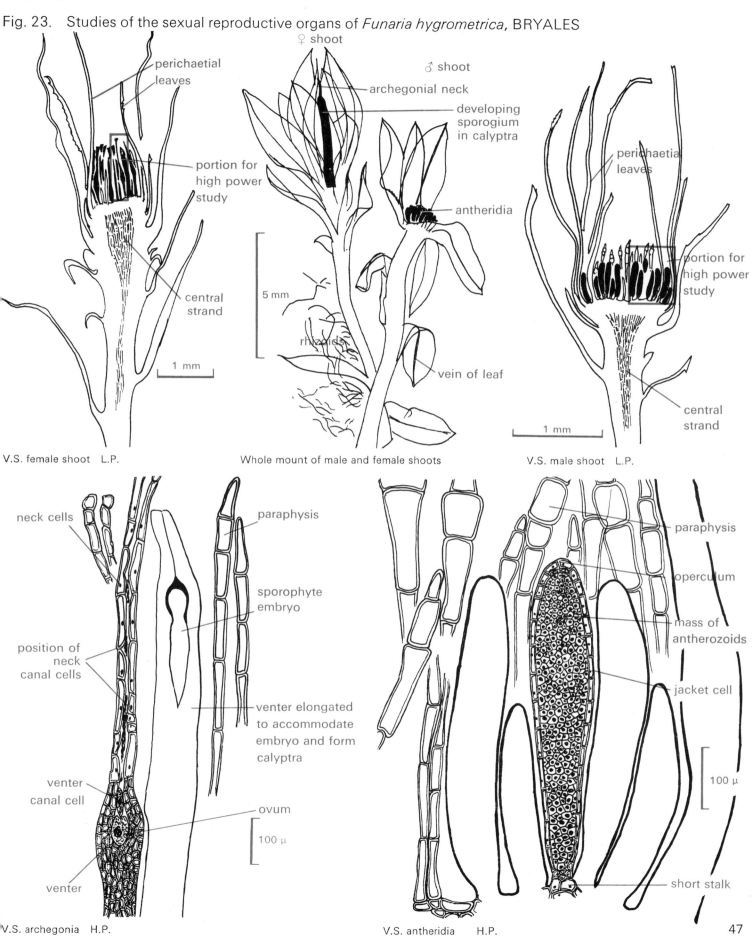

V.S. female shoot L.P.

Whole mount of male and female shoots

V.S. male shoot L.P.

V.S. archegonia H.P.

V.S. antheridia H.P.

47

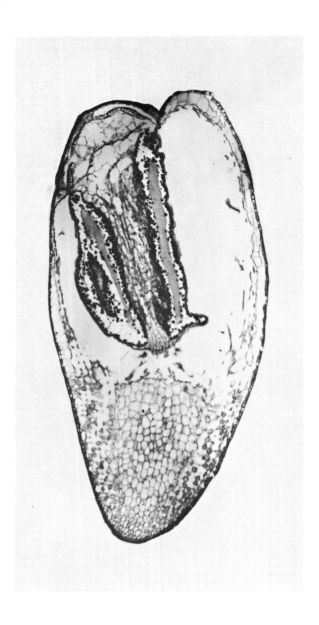

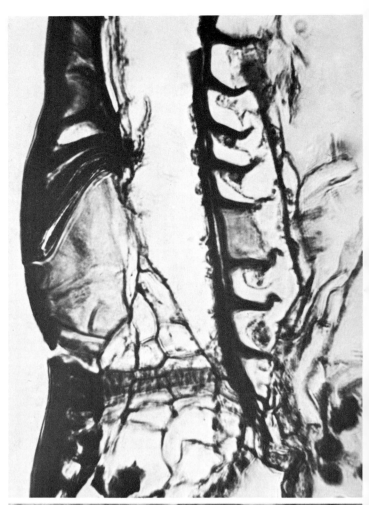

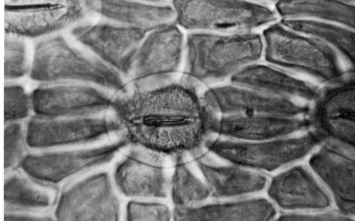

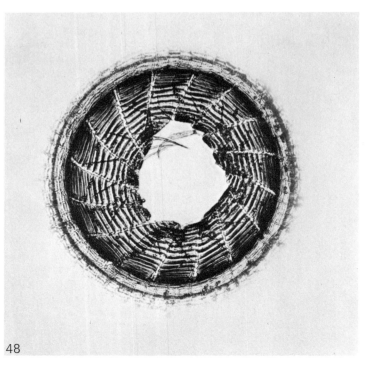

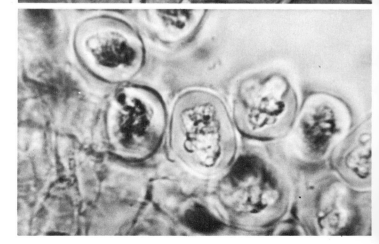

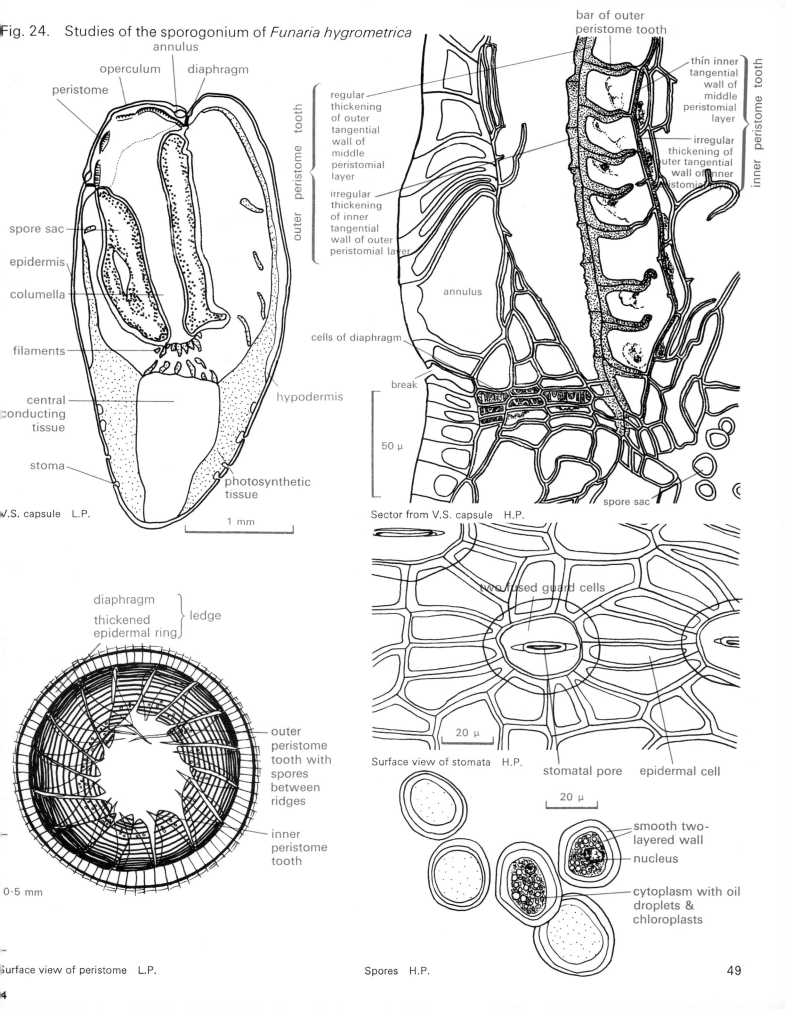

Fig. 24. Studies of the sporogonium of *Funaria hygrometrica*

V.S. capsule L.P.

peristome
operculum
annulus
diaphragm
spore sac
epidermis
columella
filaments
central conducting tissue
stoma
hypodermis
photosynthetic tissue
outer peristome tooth

1 mm

Sector from V.S. capsule H.P.

bar of outer peristome tooth
regular thickening of outer tangential wall of middle peristomal layer
irregular thickening of inner tangential wall of outer peristomial layer
thin inner tangential wall of middle peristomial layer
irregular thickening of outer tangential wall of inner peristomial layer
inner peristome tooth
annulus
cells of diaphragm
break
spore sac
50 μ

Surface view of peristome L.P.

diaphragm
thickened epidermal ring
ledge
outer peristome tooth with spores between ridges
inner peristome tooth
0·5 mm

Surface view of stomata H.P.

two fused guard cells
stomatal pore
epidermal cell
20 μ

Spores H.P.

smooth two-layered wall
nucleus
cytoplasm with oil droplets & chloroplasts
20 μ

49

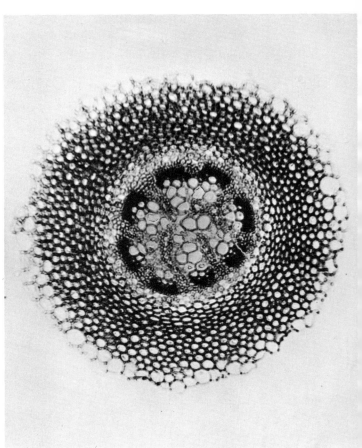

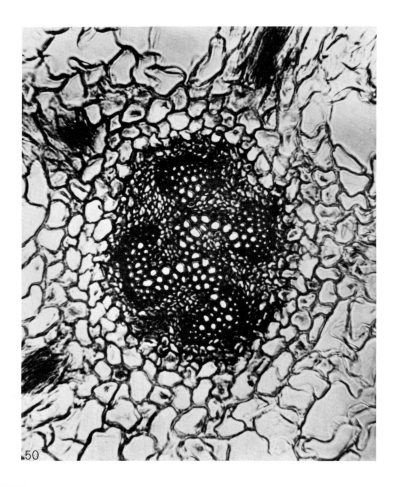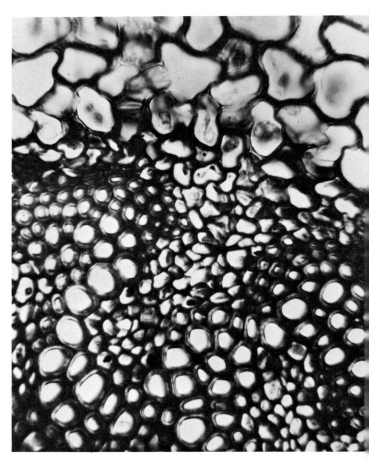

Pteridophyta-Lycopodiales

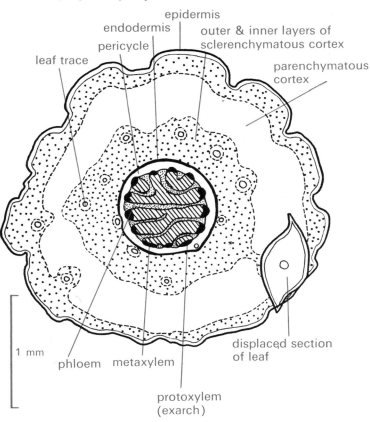

Fig. 25.   T.S. stem of *Lycopodium clavatum* (plectostele)   L.P.

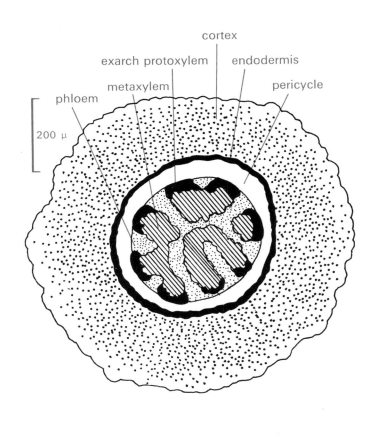

Fig. 26.   T.S. old root of *Lycopodium clavatum* (note similarity of stele to that of stem)   L.P.

Fig. 27.   T.S. stem of *Lycopodium selago* (actinostele)   L.P.

Fig. 28.   Sector from fig. 27   H.P.

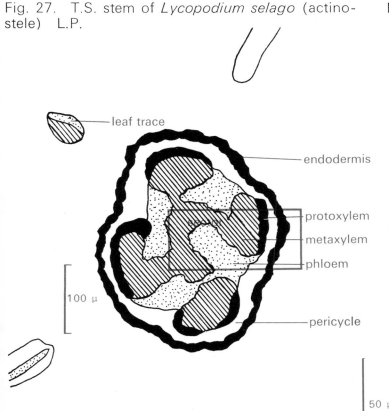

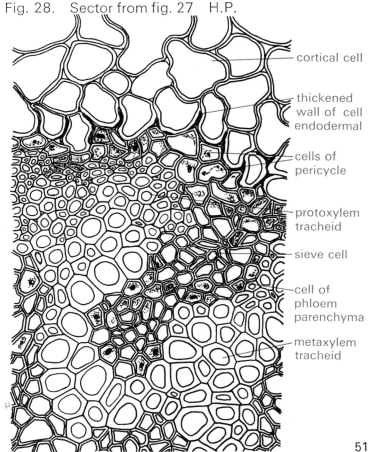

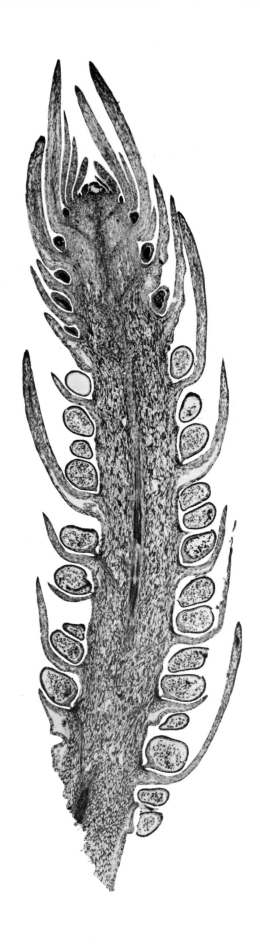

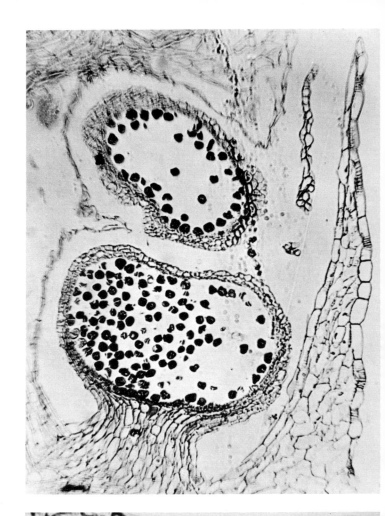

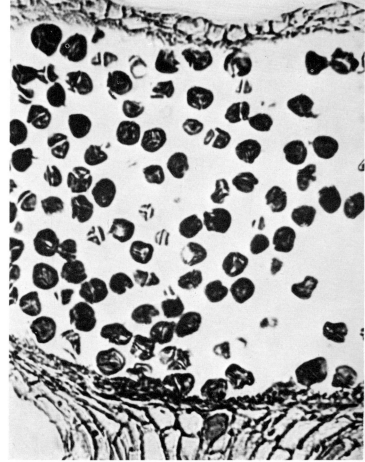

Fig. 29.   Studies of the strobilus of *Lycopodium*

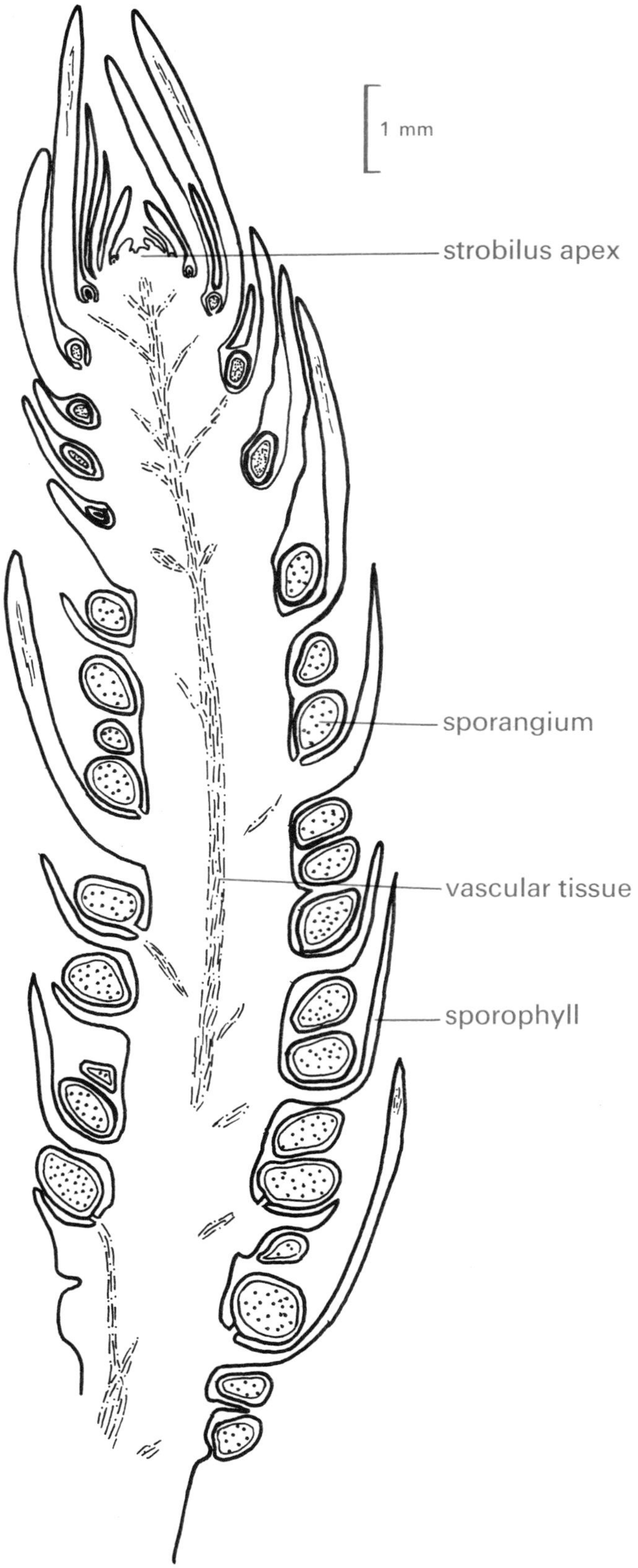

1 mm

strobilus apex

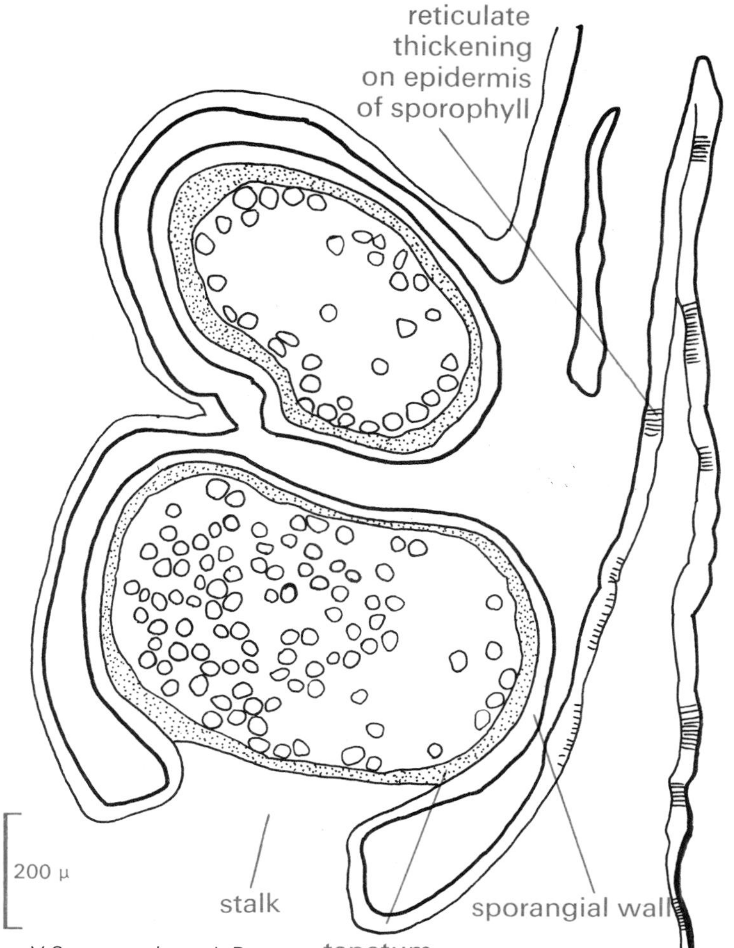

reticulate
thickening
on epidermis
of sporophyll

sporangium

vascular tissue

sporophyll

200 µ

stalk

sporangial wall

tapetum

V.S. sporangium   L.P.

thickened
wall of
sporangium

100 µ

spores

remains
of tapetum

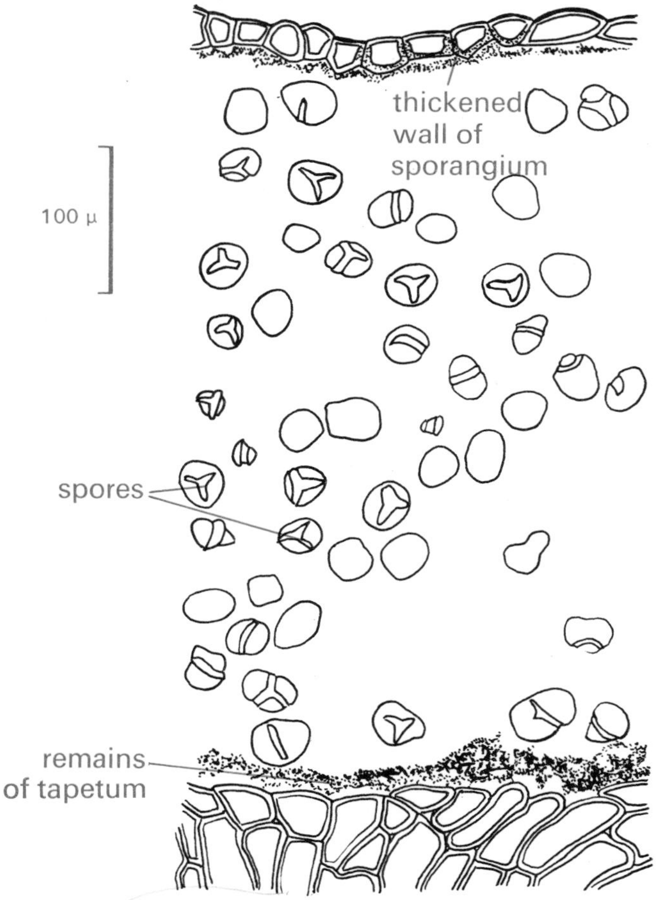

V.S. strobilus   L.P.

V.S. sporangium   H.P.

53

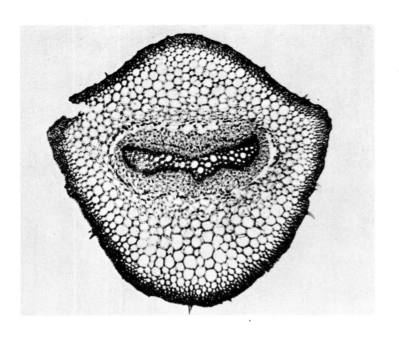

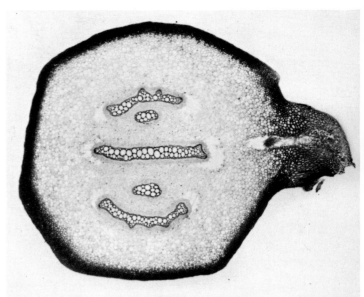

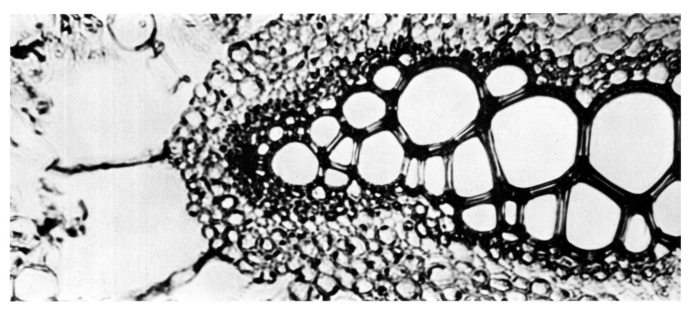

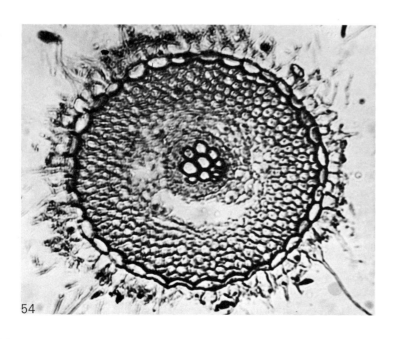

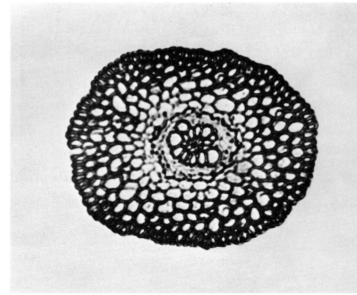

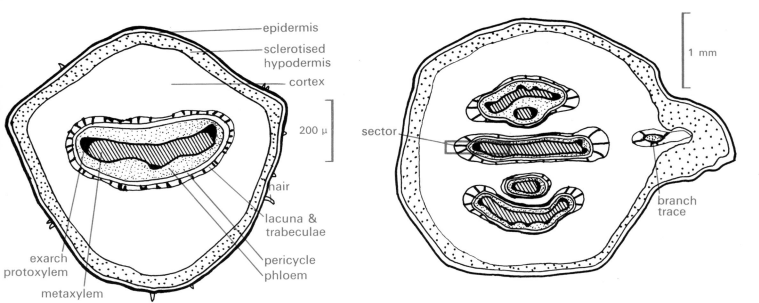

Fig. 30. T.S. stem of a monostelic species of *Selaginella* Sp. L.P.

Fig. 31. T.S. stem of a polystelic species of *Selaginella* Sp. L.P.

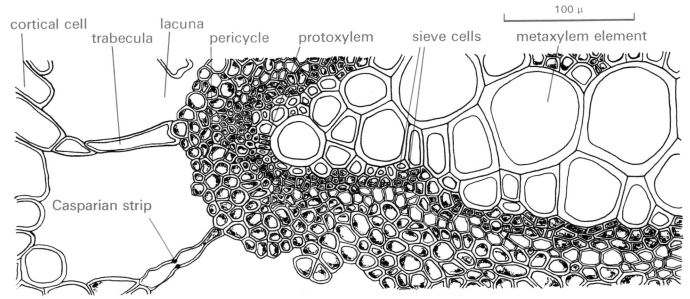

Fig. 32. Sector from fig. 31 L.P.

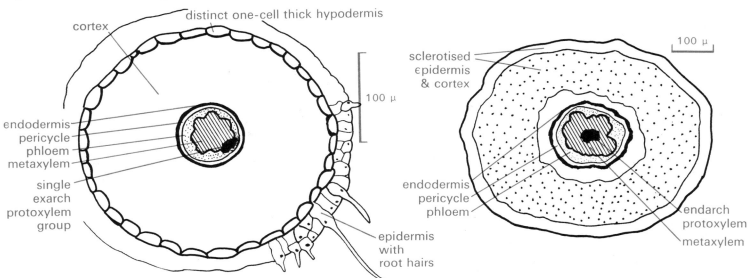

Fig. 33. T.S. root of *Selaginella* Sp. L.P.

Fig. 34. T.S. rhizophore of *Selaginella* Sp. L.P. 55

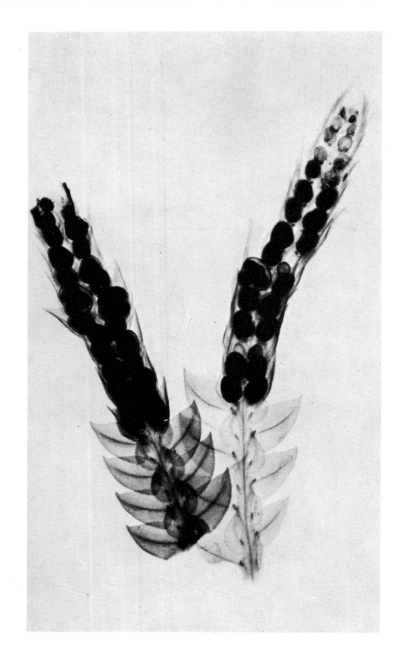

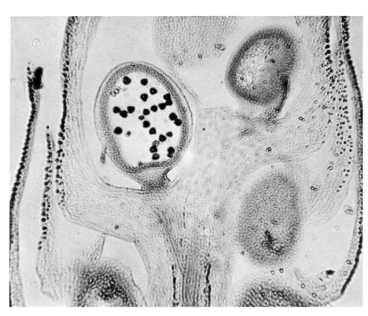

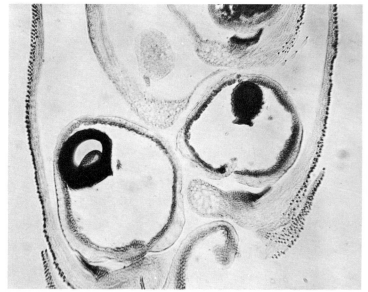

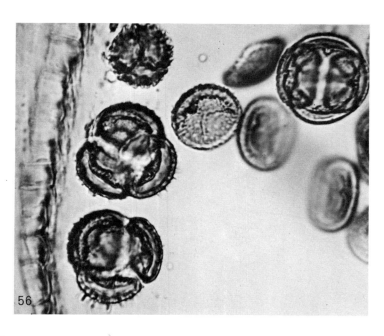

56

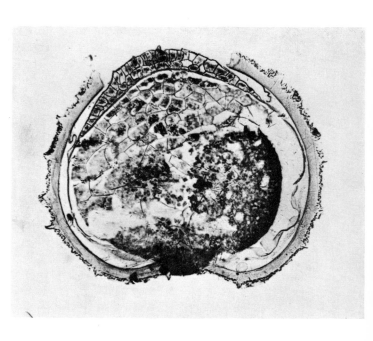

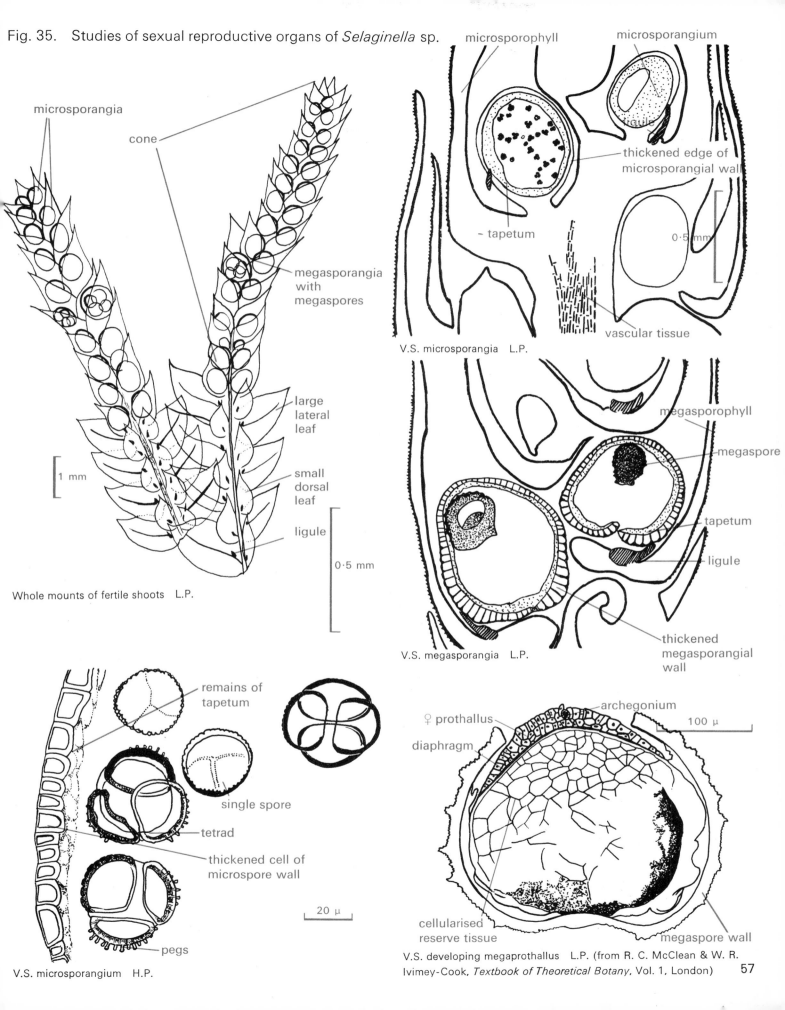

Fig. 35. Studies of sexual reproductive organs of *Selaginella* sp.

microsporangia

cone

megasporangia with megaspores

large lateral leaf

small dorsal leaf

ligule

1 mm

0.5 mm

Whole mounts of fertile shoots   L.P.

microsporophyll

microsporangium

thickened edge of microsporangial wall

ligule

tapetum

0.5 mm

vascular tissue

V.S. microsporangia   L.P.

megasporophyll

megaspore

tapetum

ligule

thickened megasporangial wall

V.S. megasporangia   L.P.

remains of tapetum

single spore

tetrad

thickened cell of microspore wall

pegs

20 μ

V.S. microsporangium   H.P.

♀ prothallus

diaphragm

archegonium

100 μ

cellularised reserve tissue

megaspore wall

V.S. developing megaprothallus   L.P. (from R. C. McClean & W. R. Ivimey-Cook, *Textbook of Theoretical Botany*, Vol. 1, London)

57

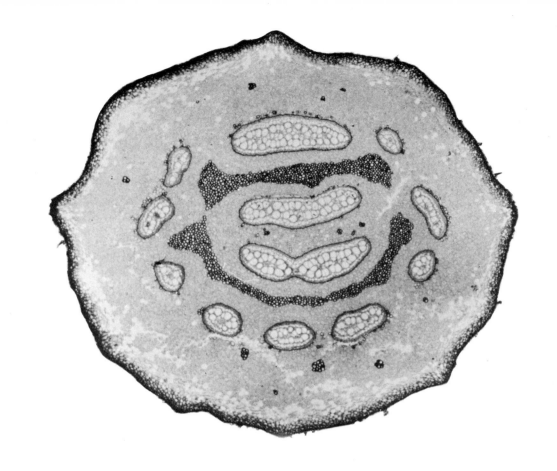

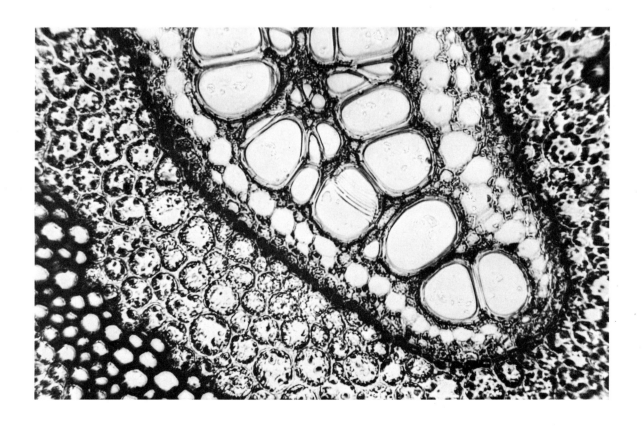

Pteridophyta-Filicales

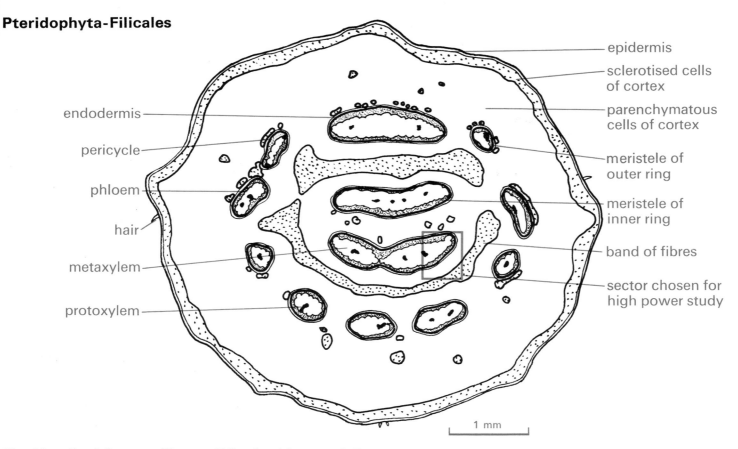

epidermis

sclerotised cells of cortex

parenchymatous cells of cortex

endodermis

pericycle

phloem

hair

metaxylem

protoxylem

meristele of outer ring

meristele of inner ring

band of fibres

sector chosen for high power study

1 mm

Fig. 36. *Pteridium aquilinum*—T.S. of a rhizome   L.P.

Fig. 37. *Pteridium aquilinum*—portion of a meristele in T.S.   H.P.

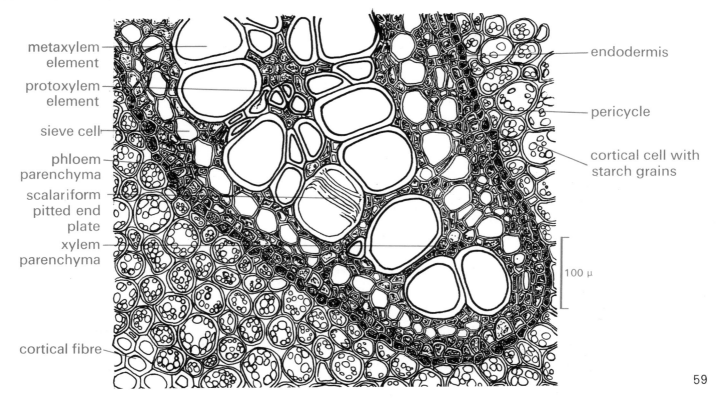

metaxylem element

protoxylem element

sieve cell

phloem parenchyma

scalariform pitted end plate

xylem parenchyma

cortical fibre

endodermis

pericycle

cortical cell with starch grains

100 μ

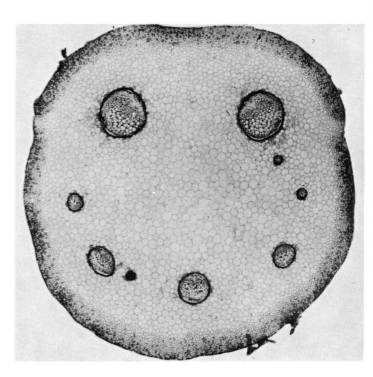

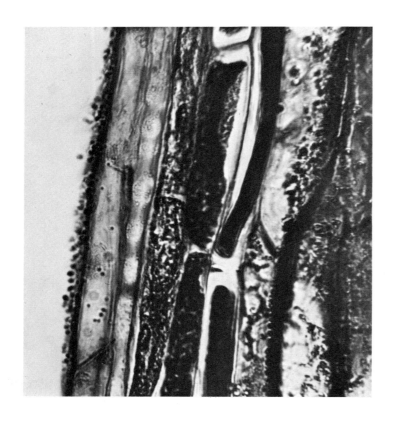

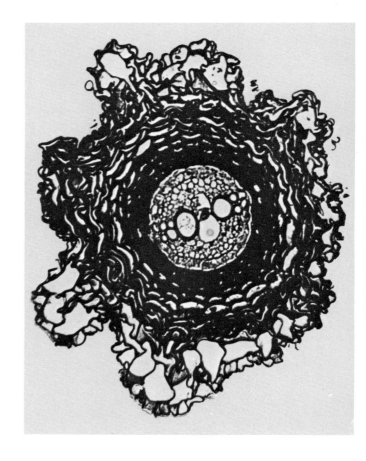

Fig. 38.   Studies of vegetative structure in Filicales

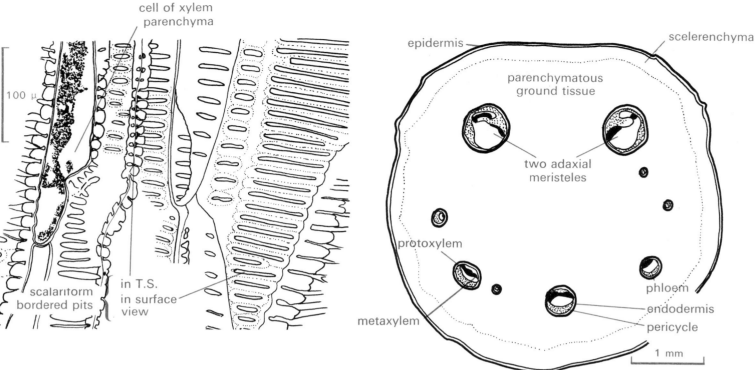

cell of xylem parenchyma

100 μ

scalariform bordered pits

in T.S.

in surface view

Pteridium—L.S. tracheids from rhizome   H.P.

epidermis

scelerenchyma

parenchymatous ground tissue

two adaxial meristeles

protoxylem

phloem

metaxylem

endodermis

pericycle

1 mm

Dryopteris--T.S. petiole   L.P.

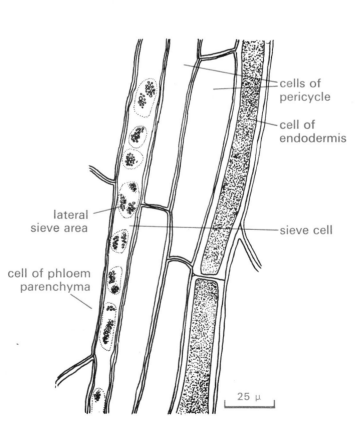

cells of pericycle

cell of endodermis

lateral sieve area

sieve cell

cell of phloem parenchyma

25 μ

Pteridium—L.S. phloem from rhizome   H.P.

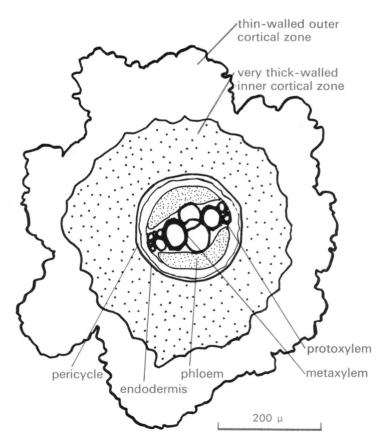

thin-walled outer cortical zone

very thick-walled inner cortical zone

protoxylem

metaxylem

pericycle

endodermis

phloem

200 μ

Dryopteris—T.S. root   L.P.

61

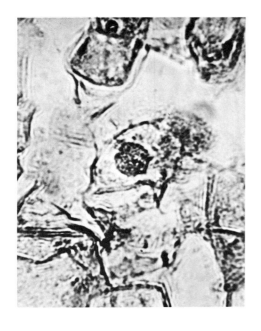

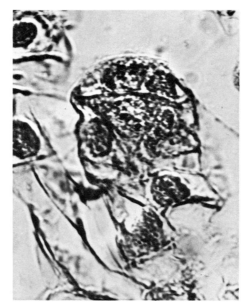

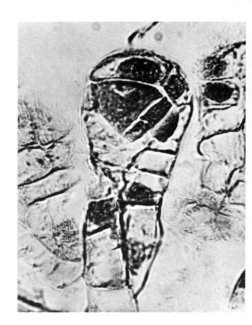

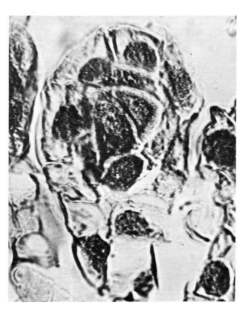

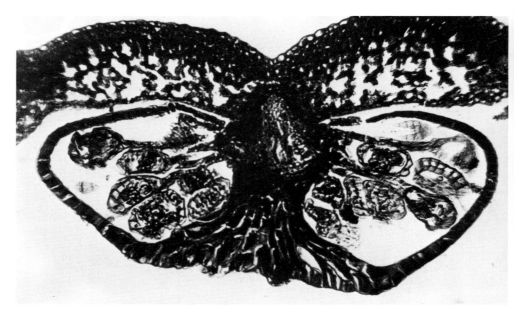

Fig. 39.   Studies of the sporangium of *Dryopteris filix-mas*

20 μ

sporangial
initial

Sporangial initiation

jacket initial

archesporial
cell

20 μ

Formation of four-sided archesporial cell

jacket initials

20 μ

tapetal
initial

stalk

First division of archesporial cell

jacket cell

one of
four
tapetal
initials

products
of first
division
of primary
sporogenous
cell

20 μ

First division of primary sporogenous cell

0·5 mm

vascular bundle

placen

indusi

annulus

sporangial capsule

V.S. sorus   L.P.

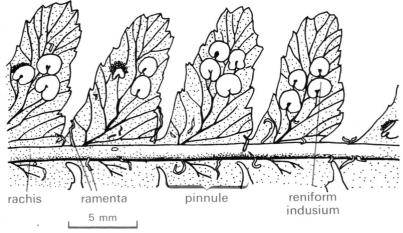

rachis   ramenta   pinnule   reniform
indusium

5 mm

Lower side of fertile pinna—living

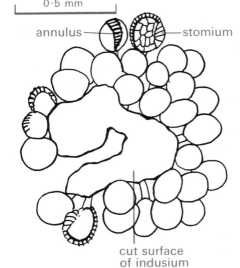

0·5 mm

annulus   stomium

cut surface
of indusium

Sorus with indusium removed—living

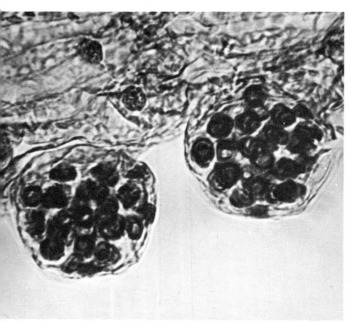
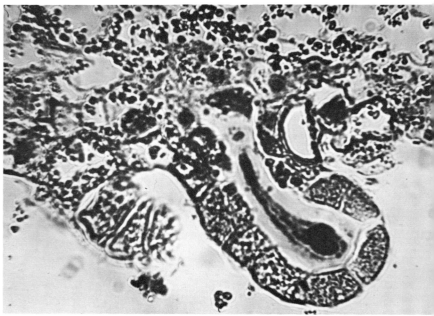

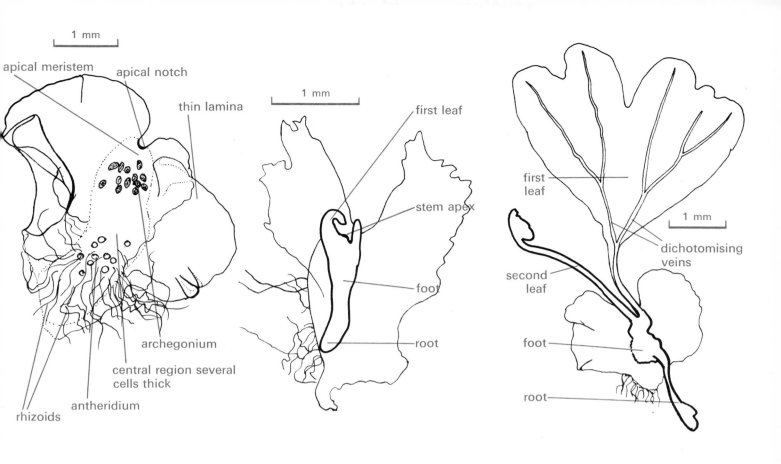

Labels for the top-left illustration:
apical meristem
apical notch
thin lamina
archegonium
central region several cells thick
antheridium
rhizoids

Labels for the top-middle illustration:
first leaf
stem apex
foot
root

Labels for the top-right illustration:
first leaf
dichotomising veins
second leaf
foot
root

1 mm

Fig. 40. *Dryopteris filix-mas*—prothallus and development of sporophyte L.P.

Fig. 41. Studies of the sexual reproductive organs of *Dryopteris filix-mas*

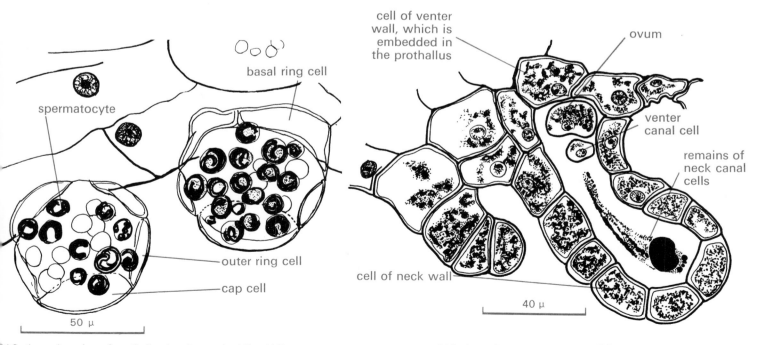

Labels for the lower-left illustration:
spermatocyte
basal ring cell
outer ring cell
cap cell

50 µ

V.S. through region of prothallus bearing antheridia H.P.

Labels for the lower-right illustration:
cell of venter wall, which is embedded in the prothallus
ovum
venter canal cell
remains of neck canal cells
cell of neck wall

40 µ

V.S. through an archegonium H.P.

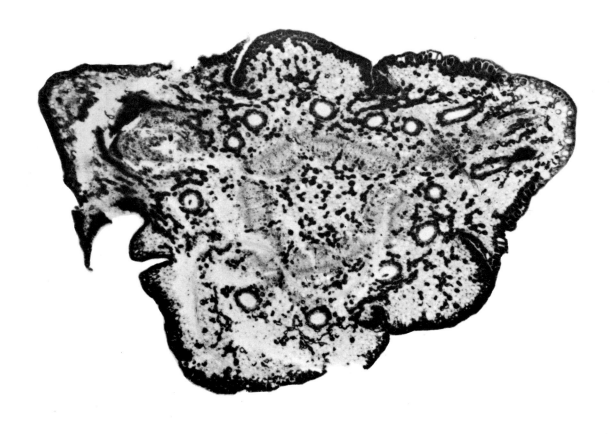

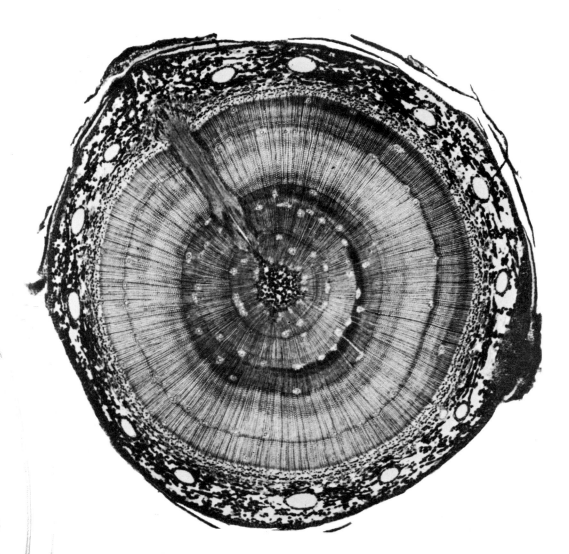

Gymnospermae

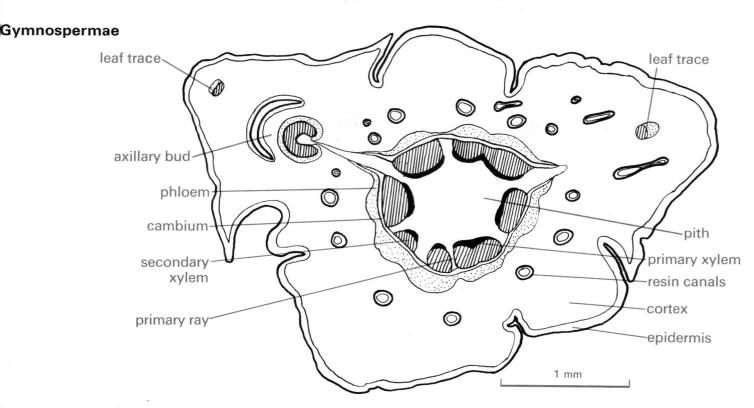

leaf trace
leaf trace
axillary bud
phloem
cambium
secondary xylem
primary ray
pith
primary xylem
resin canals
cortex
epidermis
1 mm

Fig. 42. *Pinus sylvestris*—low power study of a transverse section through a one-year-old shoot

Fig. 43. *Pinus sylvestris*—low power study of a transverse section through an old stem

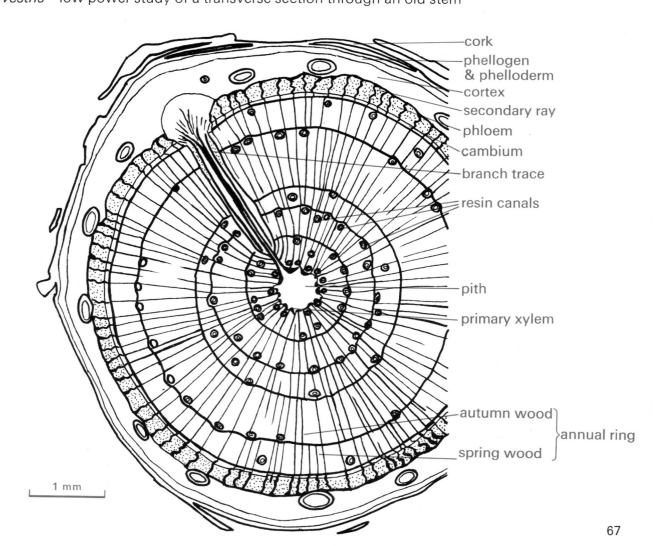

cork
phellogen & phelloderm
cortex
secondary ray
phloem
cambium
branch trace
resin canals
pith
primary xylem
autumn wood
spring wood
annual ring
1 mm

67

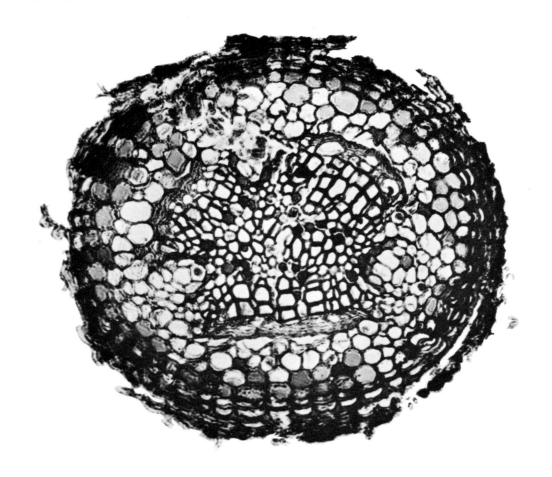

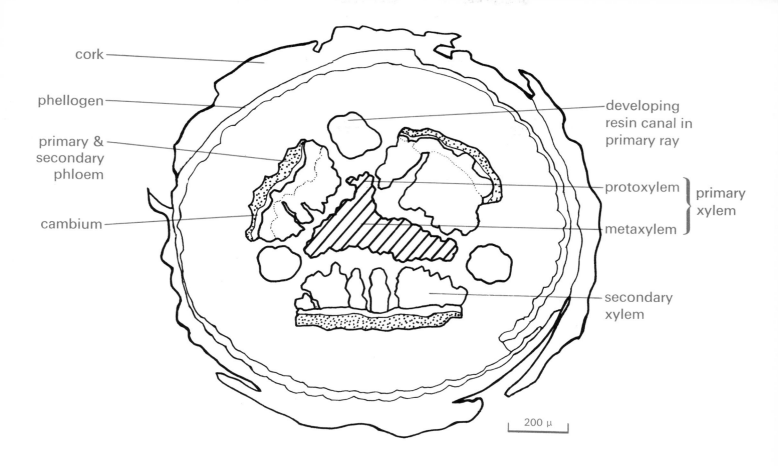

cork

phellogen

primary &
secondary
phloem

cambium

developing
resin canal in
primary ray

protoxylem ⎱ primary
            ⎰ xylem
metaxylem

secondary
xylem

200 μ

Fig. 44. *Pinus sylvestris*—T.S. of a young root   L.P.
Fig. 45. *Pinus sylvestris*—T.S. of an older root   L.P.

rhytidome

cortex

phloem

cambium

secondary ray

primary ray

resin
canals

primary xylem

secondary xylem

differentiating
secondary xylem

500 μ

69

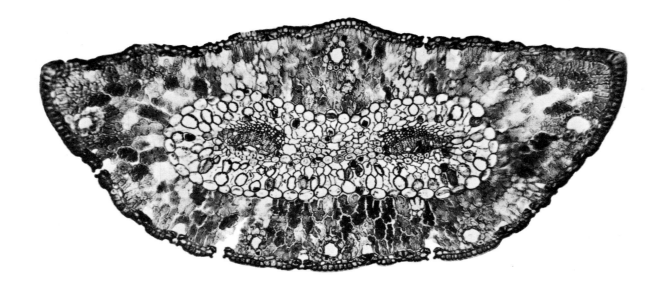

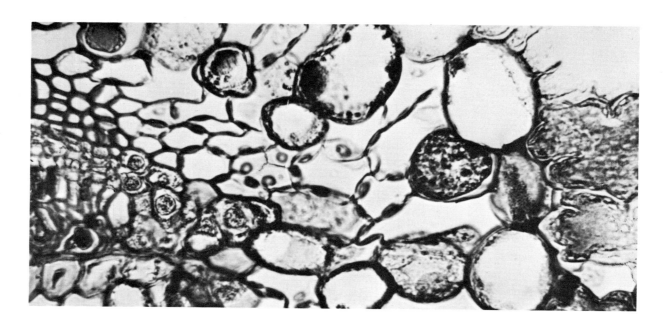

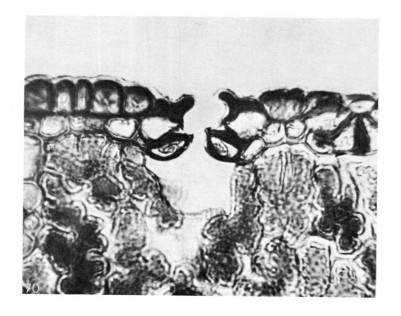

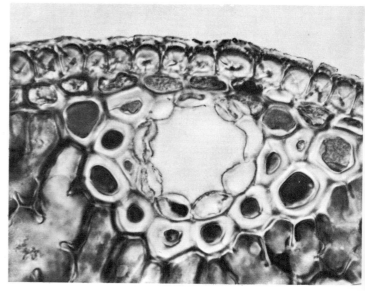

Fig. 46. Studies of the leaf of *Pinus sylvestris*

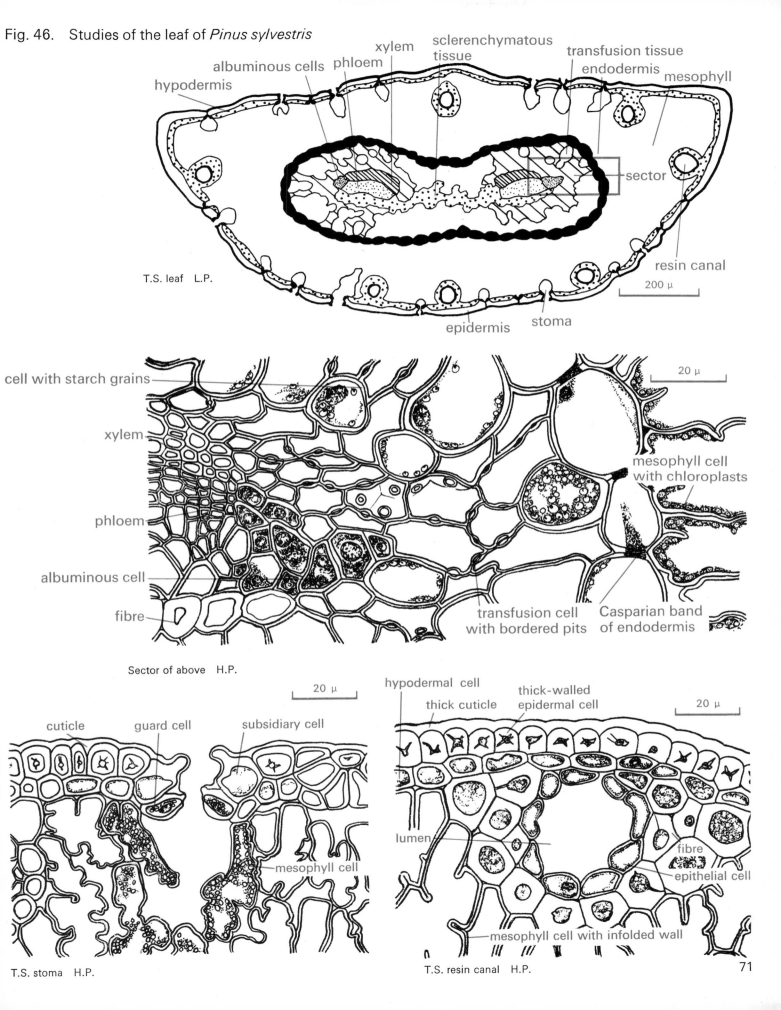

hypodermis

albuminous cells   phloem   xylem   sclerenchymatous tissue   transfusion tissue   endodermis   mesophyll

sector

T.S. leaf L.P.

resin canal

200 µ

epidermis   stoma

cell with starch grains

xylem

phloem

albuminous cell

fibre

20 µ

mesophyll cell with chloroplasts

transfusion cell with bordered pits

Casparian band of endodermis

Sector of above H.P.

cuticle   guard cell   subsidiary cell

mesophyll cell

T.S. stoma H.P.

20 µ

hypodermal cell
thick cuticle

thick-walled epidermal cell

20 µ

lumen

fibre

epithelial cell

mesophyll cell with infolded wall

T.S. resin canal H.P.

71

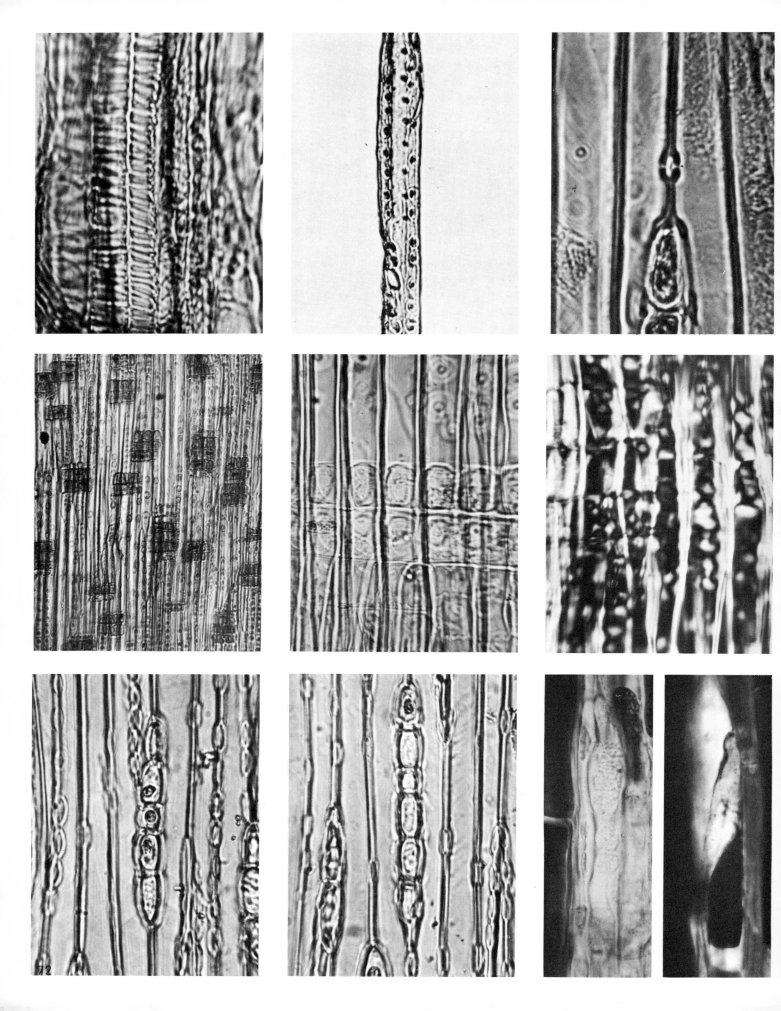

Fig. 47. Studies of the internal anatomy of the stem of *Pinus sylvestris*

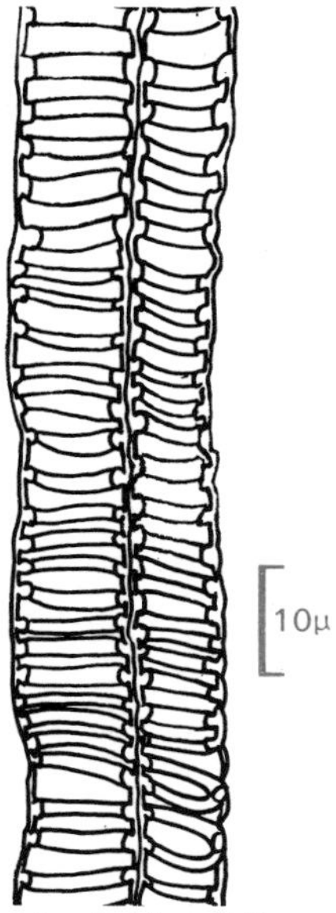

L.S. scalariform tracheids   H.P.

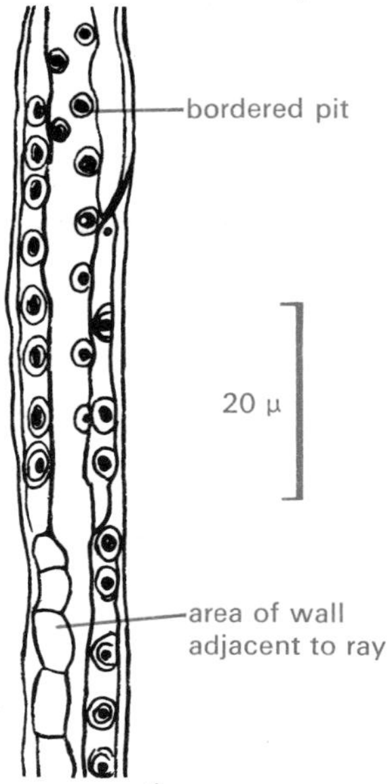

10μ

bordered pit

20 μ

area of wall
adjacent to ray

Tracheid from maceration

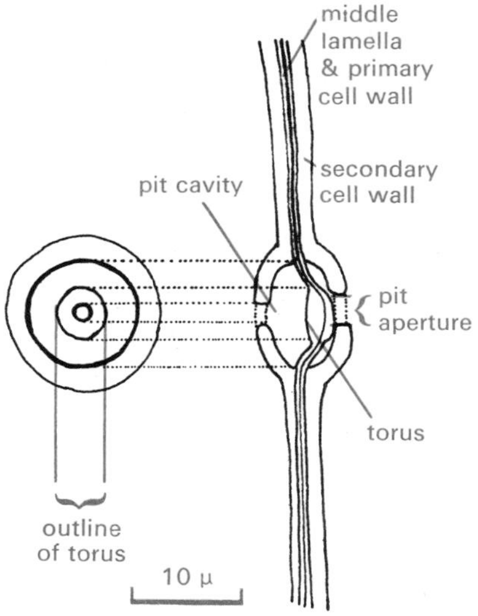

middle
lamella
& primary
cell wall

secondary
cell wall

pit cavity

pit
aperture

torus

outline
of torus

10 μ

Section and surface view of a bordered pit   H.P.
(photograph shows T.L.S. wood)

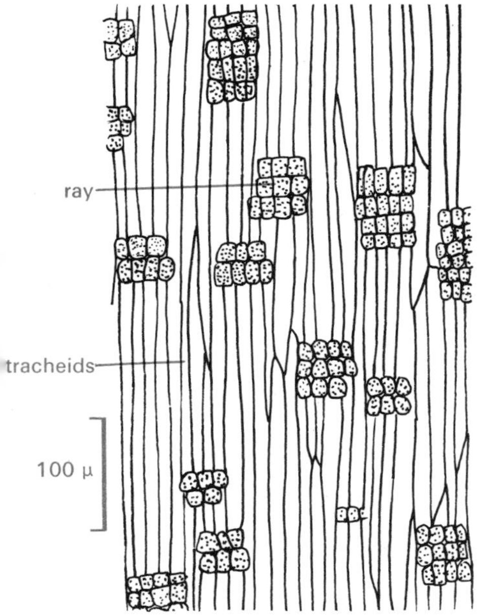

ray

tracheids

100 μ

R.L.S. wood   L.P.

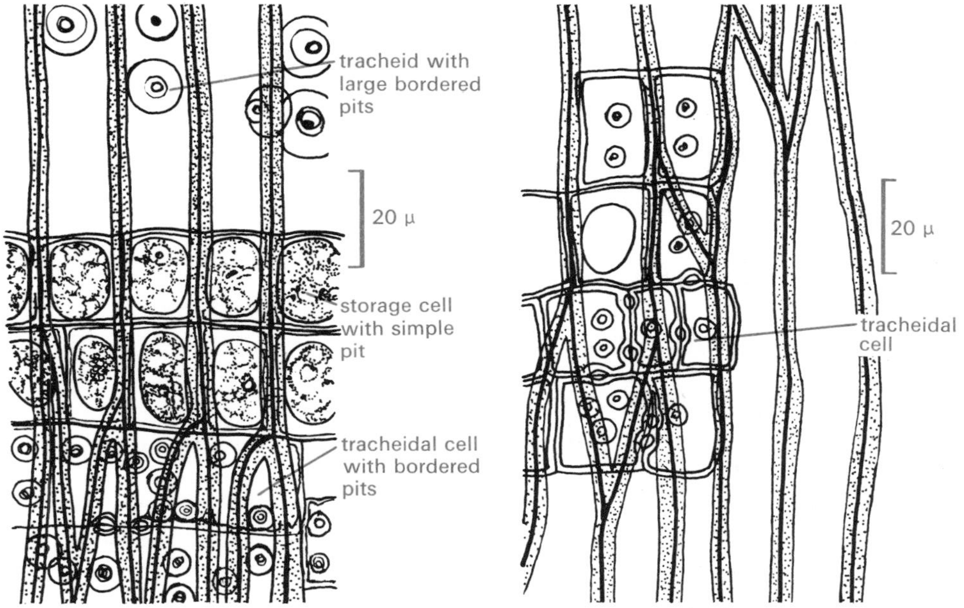

tracheid with
large bordered
pits

20 μ

storage cell
with simple
pit

tracheidal cell
with bordered
pits

R.L.S. wood   H.P. (under the light microscope and under polarised light)

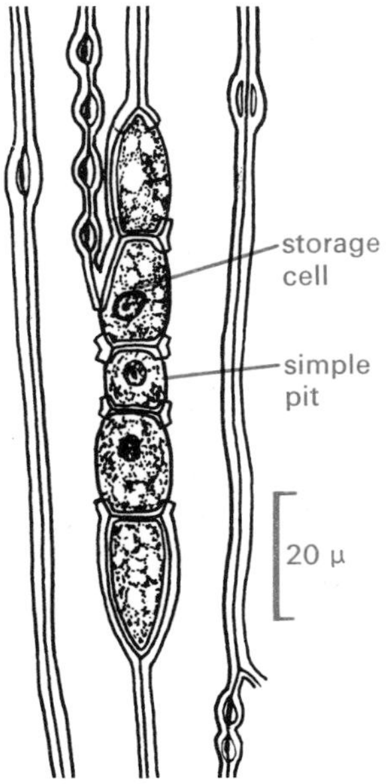

20 μ

tracheidal
cell

storage
cell

simple
pit

20 μ

T.L.S. wood   H.P.

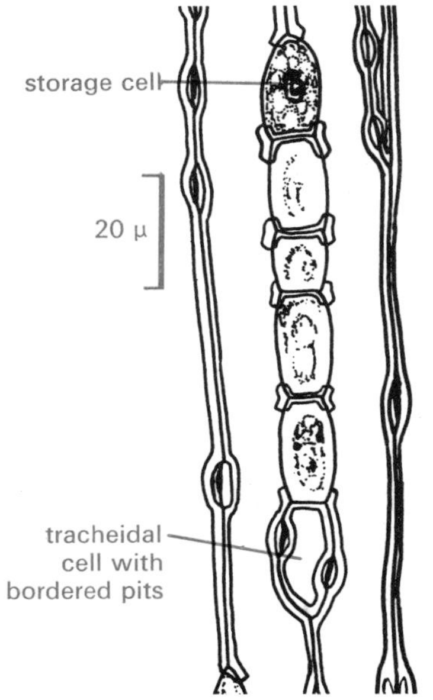

storage cell

20 μ

tracheidal
cell with
bordered pits

T.L.S. wood   H.P. (showing tracheidal cells of ray)

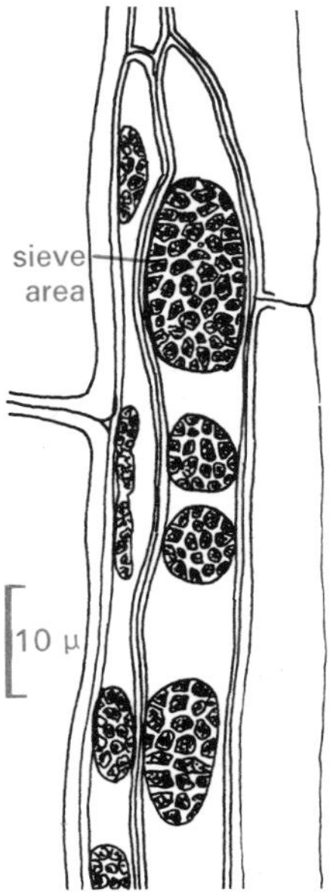

sieve
area

10 μ

sieve area
in section

10 μ

R.L.S. phloem   H.P. 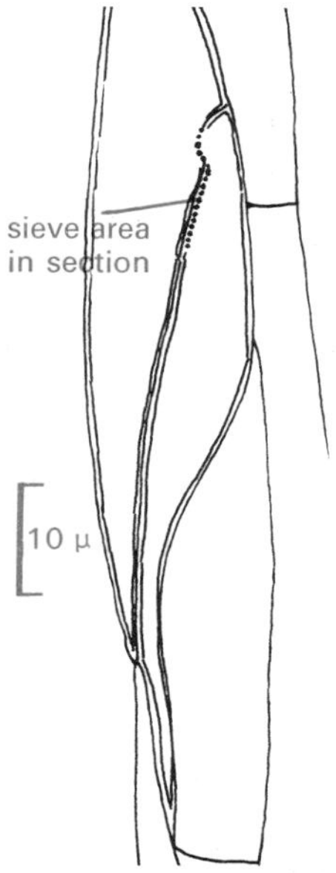   T.L.S. phloem H.P.   73

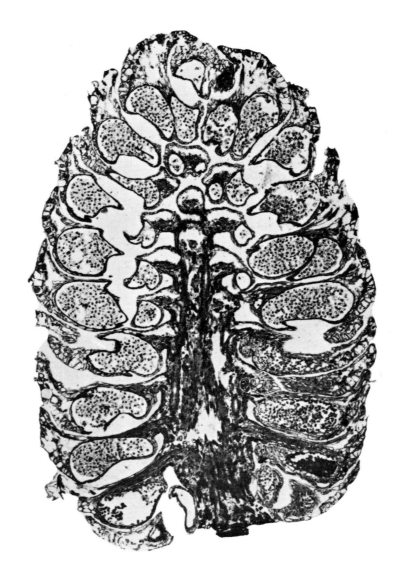

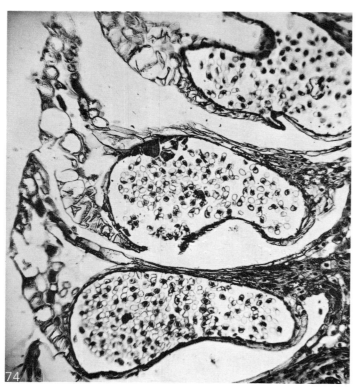

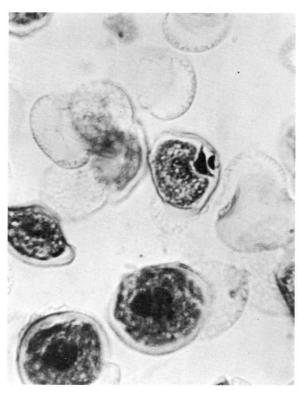

Fig. 48.   *Pinus sylvestris*—studies of a mature male cone

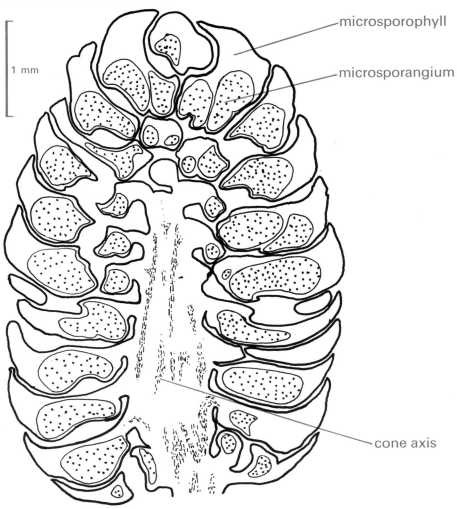

microsporophyll

microsporangium

1 mm

cone axis

V.S. mature male cone   L.P.

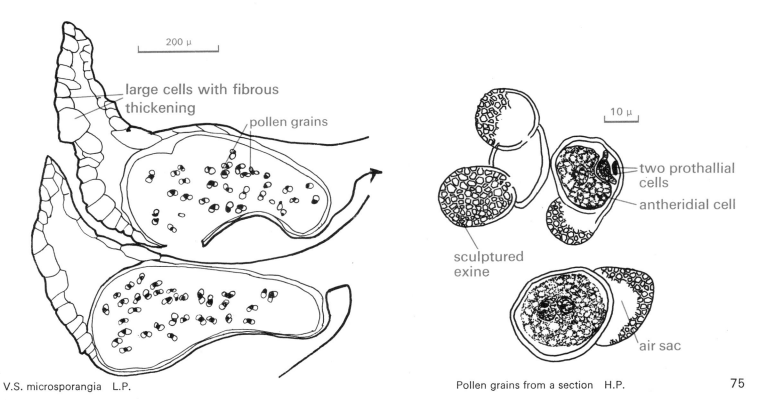

200 μ

large cells with fibrous thickening

pollen grains

10 μ

two prothallial cells

antheridial cell

sculptured exine

air sac

V.S. microsporangia   L.P.

Pollen grains from a section   H.P.

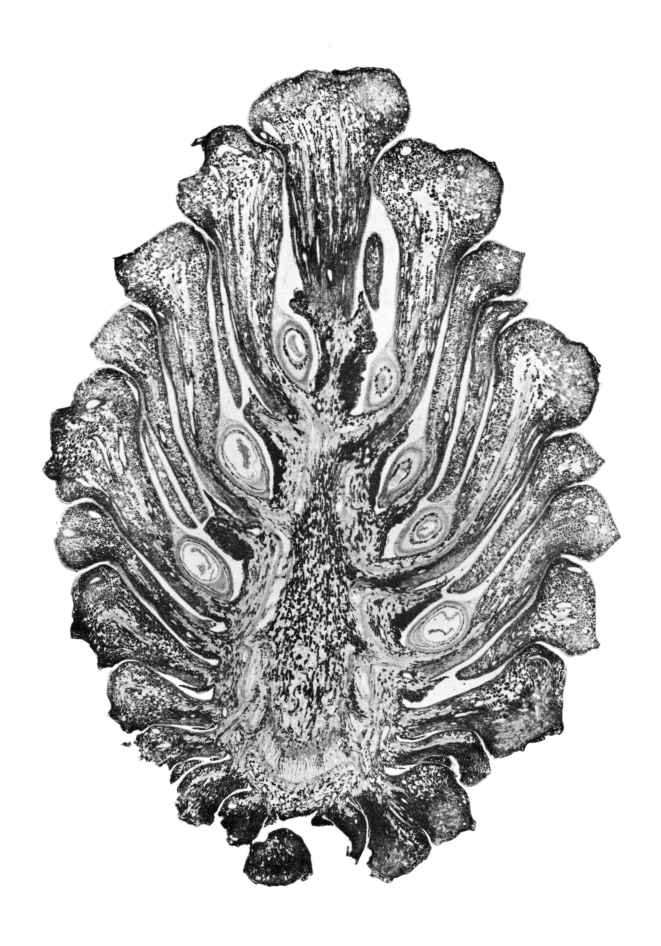

Fig. 49. Vertical section through a two-year old female cone of *Pinus sylvestris*   L.P.

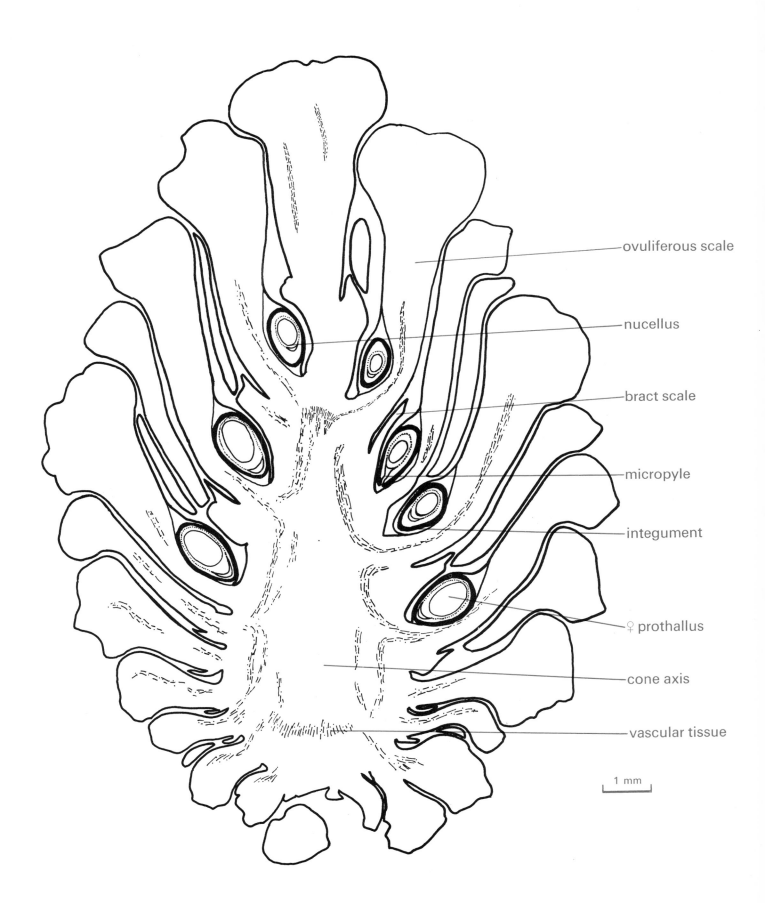

ovuliferous scale

nucellus

bract scale

micropyle

integument

♀ prothallus

cone axis

vascular tissue

1 mm

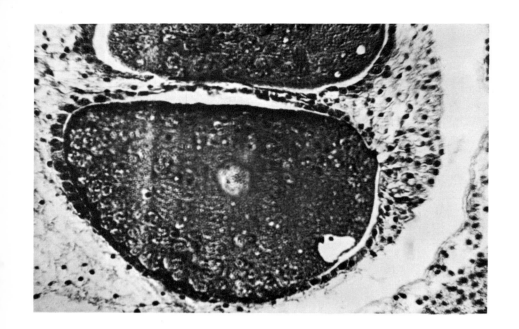

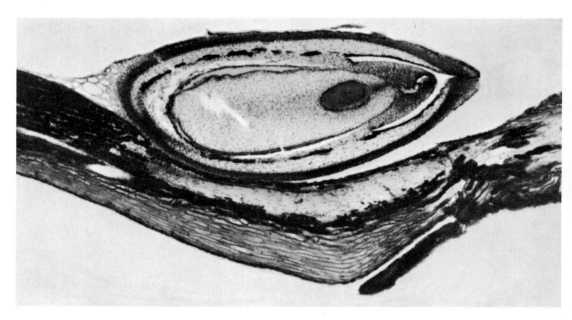

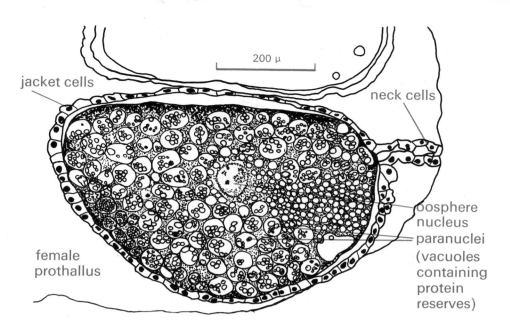

jacket cells

neck cells

200 μ

oosphere
nucleus
paranuclei
(vacuoles
containing
protein
reserves)

female
prothallus

Fig. 50. *Pinus sylvestris*—V.S. of an archegonium   H.P.

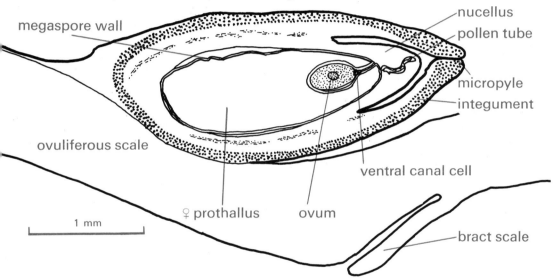

megaspore wall

nucellus

pollen tube

micropyle

integument

ovuliferous scale

ventral canal cell

♀ prothallus

ovum

1 mm

bract scale

Fig. 51. *Pinus sylvestris*—V.S. of an ovule after fertilisation   L.P.

Fig. 52. *Pinus sylvestris*—V.S. of a seed   L.P.

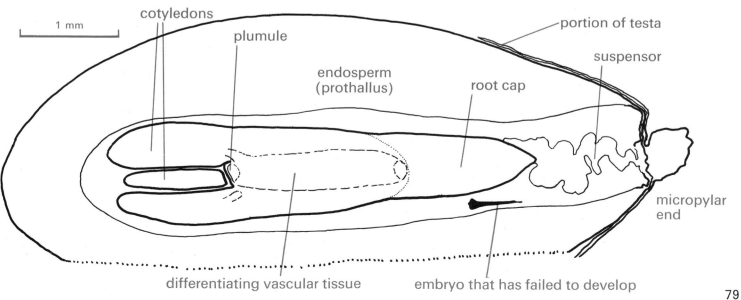

1 mm

cotyledons

plumule

portion of testa

suspensor

endosperm
(prothallus)

root cap

micropylar
end

differentiating vascular tissue

embryo that has failed to develop

Index

Algae		8–21	Musci		46 48
Ascolichenes		32	Mycorrhiza		34 36
Ascomycetes		26 28			
Aspergillus		28	*Neottia*		36
Barberry		30	*Oedogonium*		16
Basidiomycetes		28 30	Oomycetes		24
Beech		34	Orchid, Bird's Nest		36
Bird's Nest Orchid		36			
Bryales		46 48	*Pandorina*		12
Bryophyta		38–49	*Parmelia*		32
			Pellia		38 40
Chlamydomonas	vii 8	10	*Peronospora*		24
Chlorophyceae	12 14	16	Phaeophyceae		20
Cladonia		32	Phase-contrast		8 12
Conjugales		14	Phycomycetes		22 24
Cystopus		24	*Pinus*		66–79
			Pleurococcus		8
Dryopteris	60 62	64	Polarised light		72
			Psalliota		28
Ectotrophic mycorrhiza		34	*Pteridium*		58 60
Electron microscope	vii	10	Pteridophyta		58–65
Endotrophic mycorrhiza		36	*Puccinia*		30
Eudorina		12	*Pythium*		24
Euglena	vii	18			
Euglenoid movement		18	*Rhizopus*		22
Euglenophyceae		18			
Eurotium		28	*Saccharomyces*		26
			Saprolegnia		24
Fagus		34	*Selaginella*		54 56
Filicales		58–65	*Spirogyra*		14
Fucus		20			
Funaria		46 48	*Usnea*		32
Fungi		22–31			
			Vaucheria		16
Gonium		12	Volvocales		12
Gymnospermae		66–79	*Volvox*		12
Hepaticae		38–45	Wheat		30
Lichenes		32	Xanthophyceae		16
Lycopodiales		50–57	*Xanthoria*		32
Lycopodium		50 52			
			Yeast		26
Marchantia		42 44			
Marchantiales		42 44	*Zygnema*		14
Metzgeriales		38 40	Zygomycetes		22
Mucor		22			